ADULTS AND THEIR LEISURE

ADULTS AND THEIR LEISURE
The Need for Lifelong Learning

By

JOHN R. VERDUIN, JR., Ph.D.
Department of Educational Leadership
Southern Illinois University
Carbondale, Illinois

and

DOUGLAS N. McEWEN, Ph.D.
Department of Recreation
Southern Illinois University
Carbondale, Illinois

CHARLES C THOMAS · PUBLISHER
Springfield · Illinois · U.S.A.

Published and Distributed Throughout the World by
CHARLES C THOMAS · PUBLISHER
2600 South First Street
Springfield, Illinois 62717

© 1984 by CHARLES C THOMAS · PUBLISHER
ISBN 0-398-04985-8
Library of Congress Catalog Card Number: 83-24365

Printed in the United States of America
SC-R-3

Library of Congress Cataloging in Publication Data

Verduin, John R.
  Adults and their leisure.

  Includes bibliographies and index.
    1. Adult education—United States. 2. Continuing
education—United States. 3. Leisure—United States.
I. McEwen, Douglas N.   II. Title.
LC5251.V43   374'.973   83-24365
ISBN 0-398-04985-8

PREFACE

M UCH HAS BEEN WRITTEN AND SAID about two major social concepts in our academic and professional world: (1) leisure, recreation, and free-time use, and (2) adult and continuing education, or lifelong learning. Effective leisure, a positive state of mind about oneself, a good life-style, and corresponding recreational activity have received considerable note as specialists attempt to assist people of all ages to find a better state and condition of life. Attention has been given to models, propositions and theories for the very young up to the very old individual in our society. A better life, life-style, or way of living is the ultimate goal for such activity.

Another group of specialists coming from another direction wishes to help people find a better way of life too. They suggest that the continued learning of new things, ideas, concepts can help people move to a better way of living in our dynamic, troubled, and ever-changing society. Adult and continuing education or lifelong learning can help people not only to increase their earning and growing power but to find a better intrinsic way of living and enjoying life.

What would happen if these two potentially strong conceptual frameworks were combined to help people, particularly adults, seek out ways to find a better life-style, a better state of being? This particular document is an attempt to meld the two and show what might be done when one considers lifelong learning *and* leisure together in one package.

This book looks specifically at adult and continuing education, or the learning that can take place for adults. It does not negate or disregard the great potential for learning among the preadult stages, but basically addresses its attention to what can happen

v

to people at the postadolescence level in terms of effective leisure use. A need seems quite apparent that some attention should be given to adults as they seek a better life-style in this very complex society in which we are currently living.

Chapter I gives a general overview of lifelong learning, leisure, their definitions, the adult learner, and what some of the qualities of adult learning and leisure are at present. Chapter II provides a philosophical base for effective leisure use in our modern world. It offers a discussion of various benefits that can be derived from a quality leisure and recreational state of activities.

Chapter III affords some discussion on the nature of the adult and his/her life stages, characteristics, and developmental patterns and their impact on leisure and recreation behavior. A review of adult behavior and learning, or changing behavior, concludes this chapter. Chapter IV looks at current recreation models and systems that can help the adult achieve a better and more fruitful life-style. Chapter V offers some new dimensions in leisure, leisure services, and educating adults that when considered and implemented will help the adult learner move to a better state of well-being.

Chapter VI reviews some problems and issues that can confront professionals as they attempt to think through and design experiences to which adults can react and learn. Chapter VII provides some directions that lifelong learning in the leisure mode should perhaps take in order to fulfill the needs of adults.

Both of us in this writing effort have some real hope that this document will provide some help to our fellow man and his movement toward a better and more self-fulfilling life-style. We are not advocating a specific life-style, but one that is open and one that is good for each individual adult.

Although this volume is addressed primarily to the professional, the lay person can learn from it, can benefit from some of the ideas, and can, in turn, provide some much-needed leadership for the development of a sound, adult-leisure-education concept in a given community. As will be noted within, there is a significant role that lay people can play to foster and maintain this concept. Numerous councils utilize the lay person and many volunteers (some being very professional in related areas) are needed to staff an effective program in a variety of capacities. Finally, a program of good leisure learning experiences for adults may result *only* from the involvement of dedicated lay people in this particular day and age.

ACKNOWLEDGMENTS

We would like to thank many of our colleagues in our departments of Educational Leadership and Recreation for their support, advice, and encouragement in this writing project. We would also like to thank Mary Jane Schaaf, Charlene Oliver, Debra Whitaker, and Ginger Watson for their continuous effort in typing and retyping the manuscript.

Grateful acknowledgment is extended to quote from the following sources: *Leisure Today, Journal of Physical Education and Recreation*; *Adult Education* (the journal of the American Association for Adult and Continuing Education); Jean Munday and Linda Odum's *Leisure Education: Theory and Practice* (New York, John Wiley and Sons, 1979); *Parks and Recreation* (the journal of the National Recreation and Park Association); Thomas Goodale and Peter A. Witt's (eds.) *Recreation and Leisure: Issues in an Era of Change* (State College, PA, Venture Press, 1980); and *Psychology Today*. Further, we express appreciation to the Office of Intramural and Recreational Sports, Southern Illinois University—Carbondale for its work and materials on Leisure Exploration Services.

Finally, we must express our deep appreciation to our families—Janet, John, and Susan Verduin and Kiva, Rachel, and Ilana McEwen— for their continuous encouragement and support in this writing effort.

CONTENTS

ADULTS AND THEIR LEISURE

Chapter I

LEISURE AND ADULT LEARNING

Introduction

THE TERMS LEISURE AND LIFELONG LEARNING probably generate a number of ideas in the minds of people. They are both receiving considerable attention in contemporary society and are likely to generate continuous interest in the future. To offer some explanation and to bring some focus to these two major ideas, this volume will review and explore the nature of lifelong learning and the adult, the values, qualities and contributions of meaningful leisure, and other issues associated with these two potentially useful ideas. Then it will offer some suggestions as to what might be done to blend the two into a movement to improve the quality of life for all adults.

Lifelong learning is becoming and will continue to be a very popular concept for adults in America. As the American population continues its shift from a youthful one to a somewhat older one in the years ahead, more attention will be paid to lifelong learning and the contribution it can make to the welfare of its clients, the adult population. Adults will without a doubt need more formal and informal educational experiences to help them live fuller and more productive lives. Part of these learning experiences should fall within the general domain of leisure, self-enhancement, self-enrichment, and recreation.

This area of leisure, self-enhancement, and recreation should be defined as a major audience of lifelong learning comparable to the two other identifiable audiences; the education of the undereducated adult (what might be called literacy education for

3

adults) and the training, retraining, and continuing professional education of adults (vocational-occupational training and/or enhancement). Although it is the least populated of the three major audiences of thrusts in terms of participation, it can and must contribute to the well-being of adults.

The major effort in the leisure and leisure education area will continue to be important not only because of the population shift, but because of more leisure time and the need to assist adults to use leisure time more productively. And, lifelong learning, as it has in the other two major areas, can make this contribution to adults.

Considerable time for activities other than work, rest, and the other necessities of life is available to adults, and this time can be used by adults for the needed change of pace from the other requirements of life. This time can be termed *leisure time*.

LEISURE

The word *leisure* is the subject of varied interpretations and numerous definitions. It can refer to a block of time, for example leisure hours, or it can refer to activities, for example leisure pursuits. It can also mean a state of mind, a feeling of well-being and happiness. Using the latter definition one might say leisure gives direction or meaning to one's life-style. The word *leisure* comes from the Latin word *licere*, which means to be permitted. This root word has evolved into another word, license. The root word *leisure* literally meant exemption or permission as applied to the obligations of occupation. Thus leisure might be viewed as time permitted away from other essential activities. It is unobligated time or time that is not needed for existence, which includes time for eating, sleeping, and other bodily care, and also time not needed for subsistence, which includes making a living or preparing to make a living (schooling). It is a form of discretionary time when other than existence activities prevail. Kraus offers a definition that includes the concept of free time but also suggests other dimensions as well.

> Leisure is that portion of an individual's time which is not devoted to work or to other forms of maintenance activity and which therefore may be regarded as discretionary or unobligated time.
>
> Leisure implies freedom of choice, and must be seen as available to all, whether they work or not. Leisure is customarily used in a variety of ways, either to meet one's personal needs for self-enrichment, relaxation, or pleasure, or to contribute to society's well-being.[1]

While the concept of leisure as unobligated time is easily understood and readily adopted, recent critics in the recreation profession have begun to point out deficiencies in this concept. The notion of free time diverts our attention from the problems that free time cannot resolve. "Free time unavoidably carries with it a connotation of subservient worth and value. . . . It is undermined by its own definition; it is unobligated time and it is free from work. But who is ever free from work and other obligations? Because one has some discretion about how his or her time may be used does not make it unobligated."[2] Indeed time, as raw minutes, hours, and days, is a valueless concept. Free time is really only an opportunity to exercise personal choices and it is this choosing process that leads to personal value. Why not speak directly to these values in our definition of leisure? The Greeks employed the term *okole*, which evolved into words such as school and scholar, to describe the process of choice and action. The Romans employed the term *optium*, contemplation, in the same sense. Neither word has any reference to time; from this we can infer that these cultures focused on the content and value of free time pursuits.

Casting leisure within the concept of free time is objectionable because of the close relationship between time and the work rhythm. James Murphy states that "The glorification of work owing principally to the Industrial Revolution led to the separation of work and leisure, and an emphasis on economically productive functions as the most significant aspects of life, with the eventual

---

[1]Kraus. Richard. *Recreation and Leisure in Modern Society*. Santa Monica. Calif.. Goodyear Publishing Co.. 1978. p. 44.

[2]Goodale. Thomas. "If Leisure is to Matter." in *Recreation and Leisure: Issues in an Era of Change*. Thomas Goodale and Peter A. Witt (eds). State College. PA. Venture Press. 1980. p. 43.

relegation of leisure to the status of 'spare time.' "[3]

If our society ascribes to the premise that one's work is the primary determining element of all other aspects of one's everyday life, then leisure assumes a dependent role within which free individual choices are less possible. Indeed, it is clearly evident that many hard-working individuals mold their recreation patterns to fit requirements of their work life, not only in their scheduling decisions but also in their activity selections. A free time concept of leisure easily leads to a productive attitude towards the use of free time. In the work world time is money, and not working means giving up the opportunity to earn more income. The trade-off, of course, is between more income and the opportunity to freely pursue chosen activities. However, this marketplace mentality puts pressure on the individual to accomplish something of personal value during free time in exchange for the value of the lost income. Consequently, many individuals approach their leisure with the same productive attitude they approach work, packing the free hours with as many activities as will yield the maximum pleasure. Rarely encountered is the individual who will admit, after a two-week vacation, that they simply "did nothing." Unfortunately for the champions of the marketplace approach to work and leisure, keeping busy and being productive during free time does not bring profound satisfaction. At best the free-time view of leisure leads to a concept of simple amusement, a diversion from the everyday beat of the work rhythm.

Mankind was not born only to work, to march to the beat of the work rhythm of modern industrial civilization. It is interesting to note that the clock was the first fully automatic machine of the industrial revolution. Time, in terms of minutes, hours, and days, is an artificially created, culturally reinforced concept designed to meet the requirements of the industrial productive process. The natural world, of which mankind is still a part, organizes around seasons and other repeating patterns unrelated to clock time. It is

---

[3]Murphy, James F., "An Enabling Approach to Leisure Service Delivery," in *Recreation and Leisure: Issues in an Era of Change*, Thomas Goodale and Peter A. Witt (eds.), State College, PA, Venture Press, 1980, p. 197.

this natural perspective that leads toward a concept of leisure centered on personal values and personal well-being.

Sebastian de Grazia has defined leisure as a state of being in which activity is performed for its own sake or as its own end.[4] David Gray, employing the word recreation instead of leisure went on to describe this state of being:

> Recreation is an emotional condition within an individual human being that flows from a feeling of well-being and self satisfaction. It is characterized by feelings of mastery, achievement, exhilaration, acceptance, success, personal worth, and pleasure. It reinforces a positive self image. Recreation is a response to aesthetic experience, achievement of personal goals, or positive feedback from others. It is independent of activity, leisure (free time) or acceptance.[5]

While such a concept of leisure is complex and admittedly difficult to comprehend, it does focus directly on personal experiences and personal values that make leisure important to us.

Enjoyment, happiness, and satisfaction are all leisure values which enrich the adult life-style. Creativity is another important leisure value that can be experienced by the adult, a unique individual personality. Individual expression can enhance life for the adult who may have little other opportunity in everyday working and living for creative experience.

Other leisure values such as mental growth and learning, physical development, and social development can also be gained through meaningful free-time activities. Physical, mental, and social expression and interaction are important in the development and maintenance of an adult's personality. Naturally, the escape from possible boredom, standardization, and regimentation of everyday living is another leisure value. Leisure is the result of moving away from more serious and pressing problems of life and freely pursuing opportunities of a physical, mental, social, and creative nature that can lead to substantial self-enrichment. Dumazedier groups all these leisure values into three major functions that serve the individual: "relaxation, diversion or

---

[4]De Grazia, Sebastian, Of Time, Work and Leisure, New York, Twentieth Century Fund, 1962, p. 264.

[5]Gray, David E., "Exploring Inner Space," Parks and Recreation, 12:18–19, 1972.

broadening his knowledge, and his spontaneous social participation."[6] This would appear important to adults at least in terms of lifelong learning, and leisure education can foster many of these values.

In thinking of leisure, the state of well-being, we must also think of action, the act of doing well that leads to leisure. *Recreation* and *play* are the two terms that describe action and mark the pathway to leisure. Like *leisure*, both these terms are also the subject of varied interpretations and definitions. They range in meaning from physical motion such as sports and games, to mental delights such as reading or listening to music. Recreational activities must not be stereotyped as organized physical games; even the term *play*, which is associated strongly with the pursuits of children, can describe serious nonphysical activities.

Many scholars and recreational professionals have debated the terms of leisure, recreation, and play without arriving at a consensus of meaning. However, the first step in exploring the possibility of leisure education is to assign some consistent meaning to these terms. Therefore, for purposes of clarity and understanding, *leisure* will be defined as a state of well-being, of feeling good about one's life-style. *Recreation* and *play* will be defined as a series of active or passive pursuits, occurring during free time, that lead to leisure. In this context, recreation and play are viewed as a mode of action, a pathway that leads to the leisure state. Formal and informal lifelong learning can be a vehicle to help adults achieve this state.

LIFELONG LEARNING

Lifelong learning or learning beyond the usual K–12 span of activities, has a definite role to play in this much-needed area of human learning. Lifelong education or adult and continuing education might be defined as anything that can be taught to an adult in any organized informal or formal plan of education to assist the adult in doing something better about his occupational opportunities, his personal happiness, and the enhancement of

---

[6]Dumazedier, Jaffre. *Toward a Society of Leisure.* New York, The Free Press, 1967, pp. 16–17.

his social environment. It can serve adults from sixteen years of age who are not in school to those who are very much senior citizens; it is currently influencing more than 40,000,000 adults in a variety of ways and in a number of institutions, organizations, and agencies.

Adult and continuing education institutions and organizations have the ability to move quickly to meet the needs of adults in a variety of ways. These institutions have a history of meeting defined needs and interests and in helping adults move to a higher level of personal satisfaction; such has been done by them in the general area of leisure education and leisure enjoyment. However, numerically this major area falls far short of the other two major areas, and it appears that mostly retired people, spouses not on the labor market, the well-educated, and those not advancing up the career ladder are the kinds of people who participate in adult education learning experiences in leisure and recreation.

The motivational atmosphere for learning in adult education institutions reflects quite strongly the economic variable and the desire for occupational upward mobility. Adults engage in continued learning generally for job advancement, for getting a new job, or for improving personal income. Leisure education concerns thus find themselves low on the priority list. Further, the adults who participate in all of the formal adult and continuing education experiences seem to be quite educated, middle-class, and young. Adult education does less well for lower income, less-educated, elderly, and minority people. In general, the lifelong learning adult also is a voluntary and part-time student who is employed full-time and who pays for the continued schooling. These facts definitely have implications when thinking about leisure, lifelong learning, and education.

Leisure education, a major phase of lifelong learning, should be the delivery system that will enhance the individual and improve the quality of life for the adult. It is much broader than just offering some forms of recreation and recreation services, and more than learning some sports skills that may be used on weekends. It has to be individually oriented "to enable individuals to enhance the quality of their lives in leisure."[7] An adult must be guided to look at and clarify important values, attitudes, and goals of leisure, and must decide what the state-of-being leisure will develop in his/her lifestyle. It should be so designed to help develop the potential of individual adults to help themselves in doing a better job in the selection of leisure alternatives. It has to involve a number of disciplines and delivery systems to be effective, and it should be "a lifelong, continuous process encompassing prekindergarten to retirement years."[8] Although the early years of education are very important, the major focus of this volume is the postsecondary leisure education experiences.

Lifelong Learning Institutions and Leisure

A number of agencies and organizations exist that can deliver the learning experiences in the area of leisure to adult clients. To fulfill the leisure needs of adults, four major categories of delivery systems exist that can assist the adult. Public agencies and institutions that are supported by governmental bodies at the federal, state, and local levels are major contributors to leisure and leisure education. These would include recreation and park districts, numerous educational institutions, community centers, and sports facilities and agencies. Instruction can occur in a variety of major areas within publicly supported agencies and institutions.

The second and third major delivery systems, voluntary group work agencies and private groups, do provide for the leisure needs of adults but mostly on a restricted membership-only basis. In these two categories, adult learning can take place in such organizations as churches, social, fraternal, and service clubs, YMCA/YWCAs, and business and industry and generally take place as needs arise among the membership.

The final contributor, commercial recreational enterprises, is designed to make a profit from its services and provides some adult instruction. These enterprises afford instruction to

---

[7]Mundy, Jean and Linda Odum. *Leisure Education: Theory and Practice.* New York. John Wiley & Sons. 1979. p. 3.

[8]Ibid. p. 3.

those adults who wish the kinds of leisure opportunities offered by the numerous companies. This latter category results in a multibillion dollar industry in America.

SELF-DIRECTED ADULT LEARNING

Although considerable learning in leisure and leisure use takes place in various sponsoring institutions, agencies, and organizations, adults can and do learn many things about their world in a self-directed and self-planned manner. For example, if a person wished to learn about macrame and apply that knowledge to the construction of a specific form, the learner may decide to enroll in some formal adult class and gain the appropriate skills and knowledge and proceed. Or, the adult learner may check out some books at the local library, review the processes involved, and proceed to construct the form. Or, the adult learner may discuss the process with a friend, review some books and pamphlets and proceed. The latter two efforts would fall under the category of self-directed learning, personal learning not under the direction or guidance of some professional in an agency or institution.

Allen Tough suggests that about 70 percent of adult learning falls in the self-directed and self-conducted category while about 20 percent comes under the direction of a professional person in an institution of some sort; the remaining learning time comes from working under the guidance of friends and/or acquaintances and from working within a democratic group of peers.[9] This rather astounding figure offers kind of an iceberg effect in terms of total adult learning in America. The top of the iceberg shows about 20 percent of the total adult learning occurring in such places as community colleges, evening public schools, YMCAs, and other quite obvious places while the remaining 70 to 80 percent of adult learning is not really visible to the adult educator's eye. This kind of adult learning has great significance to leisure use and leisure education, since the typical adult can spend

---

[9]Tough, Allen, *Major Learning Efforts: Recent Research and Future Directions,* Ontario, Ontario Institute for Studies in Education, 1977.

about 100 hours a year on a learning effort and participate in five major learning experiences in a year. Much of this resulting 500 hours of learning is done through self-direction and self-planning, while some is planned by amateurs such as peers and friends.

A learning effort or learning project "is a highly deliberate effort to gain and retain certain definite knowledge and skills, or to change in some way."[10] Usually a series of related learning experiences should add up to at least seven hours. This definition includes the wide range of major learning efforts such as attending a class, reading, observing, practicing, and getting answers to questions. It is estimated that 90 percent of all adults conduct at least one learning effort a year, with the most common motivation, as might be expected, being that of some anticipated use or application of the knowledge or skill. Less common motivators might be curiosity, puzzlement, or wanting to possess the knowledge for its own sake.

One survey revealed that most learning projects were job-related or recreational with some numbers given to personal improvement, religion, and family relations.[11] Penland found that personal development, home and family, hobbies and recreation, general education, job, religion, voluntary activity, public affairs, and agriculture/technology were the major areas of emphasis.[12] In this study it was also revealed that most adults preferred to learn in their homes, with other responses indicating the outdoors, a discussion group, a library, and public events as preferred places for learning.

Penland further delved into the reasons why people chose to learn on their own instead of taking formal courses of some sort. The desire to set one's own pace in learning was the most frequent response given, followed by a desire to use one's own style of learning, the need to keep the learning strategy flexible and easy to change, the need to learn something right now and

---

[10]Ibid. p. 2.

[11]Peters, John M. and Susan Gordon, *Adult Learning Projects: A Study of Adult Learning in Urban and Rural Tennessee,* Knoxville, University of Tennessee, 1974.

[12]Penland, Patrick R., *Individual Self-Planned Learning in America* (unpublished manuscript), Graduate School of Library and Information Sciences, University of Pittsburgh, 1977.

not wait for a class to begin, the lack of classes on the desired topic, the lack of time to get into a formal class, the dislike for a formal classroom and teacher, the lack of sufficient funds to pay for a class, and the lack of transportation with its accompanying difficulty and cost. It is interesting to note that transportation and cost were perceived as very low as the reason for learning in this particular manner.

Hiemstra did a study of older adults, people fifty-five years of age and older, in Nebraska. He found that more than half of the learning projects of people this age dealt with self-fulfillment, such as arts and crafts, recreation, and religion.[13] Other evidence from the study showed interest on the part of older adults to be along the lines of personal and family concerns, health factors, and finances. Some concerns were expressed for job improvements and social and civic competence. Further, this survey showed that those with fewer formal education experiences wished to learn on their own. While the more educated adult turns to formal classroom learning, the less educated tries to learn on his/her own because of previous unhappy school experiences.

It appears from these studies and others that the area of leisure, recreation, and self-enrichment has been identified as one where considerable self-planned and self-directed learning has taken place. This, as suggested above, has significance to the adult education professional who has interest in helping people in the areas of leisure, use of leisure, and leisure education. Adults do need guidance and assistance in this area even though they do much of the planning and learning activity on their own in the self-directed learning process. Adults move from an awareness of a general problem or issue to an expression of a need to learn something or a decision to begin some sort of learning project. Longer term objectives can be established, and then resources are identified and obtained. Movement beyond these points can then vary greatly. Perhaps the adult leisure education professional will have to assist the adult in knowing

---

[13]Hiemstra. Roger. *The Older Adult and Learning*. Lincoln. Department of Adult and Continuing Education. University of Nebraska. 1975.

how to start learning projects by the setting of goals, in defining and making time to complete the learning projects, and by defining formative and summative evaluation measures to check the success of the learning experience. Giving overall assistance and facilitating relevant learning can be critical to the self-directed adult learner. It appears that adults want help and competence with planning and guiding their very own learning experiences.

THE ADULT LEARNER

Adult learners, the recipients of lifelong learning, are very complex individuals. They go through many stages as they move from early adulthood to senior citizen status. They bring many perceptions and experiences to a leisure learning experience and their needs, interests, goals, values, and personal backgrounds vary considerably. Their social status, their available time, their social and family responsibilities, and their personal resources will all impact on their desire and commitment to leisure education activities. The young adult generally possesses full physical and mental abilities; as aging occurs, the physical abilities begin to slow down, but generally older adults have the mental abilities to cope with most learning experiences even though it may take longer to complete learning tasks. It should be kept in mind that almost any adult can learn any subject if given enough time and guidance. Their needs for continued learning, however, are truly insatiable in terms of requests; they want to learn about everything. Adults really are continuous learners in an informal way as they adjust to the many role changes that confront them in life. Much of the learning activity is directed toward the economic variable, but leisure, self-enhancement and recreation are important too. This continuous learning behavior on the part of adults is certainly an asset to the professional adult educator.

However, it appears that adults get into a leisure or recreation "rut" as they move throughout life. A kind of set pattern of activities is established early, and not many changes in leisure habits occur. At middle life there may be a decline in participation in leisure activities perhaps due to a decline in physical and mental vigor or because leisure and fun and games are believed to be "for the young." The leisure industry may be responsible for the latter reason for decline in activity. Such social inhibitions and the personal lack of inclination could account for the failure of older adults to engage in new leisure interests. Thus, from a very active and often physical leisure experience in early adulthood, the adult will move to less activity and not really experience new leisure activities. Perhaps leisure education can play a significant role in expanding the opportunities for adults of all ages.

All of these many variables are critical to consider when viewing and deciding what can and perhaps should be done to help adults live a richer life and experience a better state of being in this society. The main focus of this volume deals with adults, so much greater explication of the adult, the accompanying behaviors, and modes of changing that behavior appears in future chapters.

SUMMARY

It would appear from the above discussion that the potential for lifelong learning in the area of effective leisure and leisure use is quite significant. Adult and continuing education institutions are present that can offer those learning experiences, and more can be developed to meet the many current and emerging needs. The spirit, attitude, and philosophy are present to respond to the various needs. Further, the adult is a lifelong learner by nature and engages in many self-directed experiences throughout a given period of time. Considerable additional learning does take place on the part of adults and much of this can and should take place in using leisure to enhance the quality of life for people.

However, several factors can complicate the potential for significant learning. The massive diversity of needs, interests, and goals of adults and the insatiable appetite they have for learning things of interest can make the adult-education leisure specialist's job a very difficult one. That much institutional adult learning usually deals with the pragmatic or economic variable (job opportunities and advancements) and that learning leisure use is low on the priority list does not make it any easier. Also, self-directed adult learning deserves much greater attention to fulfill its potential. When these factors are coupled with the idea that adults appear to get locked into a recreation and leisure rut and don't easily emerge from it, the adult learning professional knows real concern.

To facilitate this important area of American education, perhaps what is needed is to educate professionals and nonprofessionals alike as to what leisure education can do for all adults and their quality of life. A rationale or philosophical base can be the starting point. Chapter II of this volume offers some philosophical considerations.

SELECTED BIBLIOGRAPHY

Bates, Barbara J. (ed.), "Leisure and Aging: New Perspectives," *Leisure Today, Journal of Physical Education and Recreation*, 48(8), 1977.

Bischof, Ledford J., *Adult Psychology*, 2nd. ed. New York, Harper and Row, 1976.

Cheek, Neil H., Jr. and William R. Burch, Jr., *The Social Organization of Leisure in Human Society*, New York, Harper and Row Publishers, 1976.

Corbin, H. Dan and William J. Tait, *Education for Leisure*, Englewood Cliff, NJ, Prentice Hall, Inc., 1973.

Damazedier, Jaffre, *Toward a Society of Leisure*, New York, The Free Press, 1967.

Davis, Joan, "Valuing: A Requisite for Education for Leisure," *Leisure Today, Journal of Physical Education and Recreation*, 47(3), 1976.

De Grazia, Sebastian, *Of Time, Work and Leisure*, New York, Twentieth Century Fund, 1962.

Dobbs, Ralph C., "Leisure as a Component of Lifelong Learning," *Lifelong Learning: The Adult Years*, 1(3), November, 1977.

Dumazedier, Joffre, *Sociology of Leisure*, Elsevier, 1974.

Elias, John L. and Sharon Merriam, *Philosophical Foundations of Adult Education*, Huntington, NY, Robert E. Krieger Publishing Co., 1980.

Godbey, Geoffrey and Stanley Parker, *Leisure Studies and Services: An Overview*, Philadelphia, W. B. Saunders Co., 1976.

Godbey, Geoffrey, *Leisure in Your Life: An Exploration*, Philadelphia, Saunders College Publishing, 1981.

Goodale, Thomas and Peter A. Witt (eds.), *Recreation and Leisure: Issues In An Era of Change*, State College PA, Venture Press, 1980.

Harrington, Fred Harvey, *The Future of Adult Education*, San Francisco, Jossey-Bass Publishers, 1977.

Heimstra, Roger, *Lifelong Learning*, Lincoln, Nebraska, Professional Educators Publication, Inc., 1976.

Iso-Ahola, Seppo E. (ed.), *Social Psychological Perspectives on Leisure and Recreation*, Springfield, IL, Charles C Thomas, Publisher, 1980.

Iso-Ahola, Seppo E., *The Social Psychology of Leisure and Recreation*, Dubuque, IA, Wm. C. Brown Company Publishers, 1980.

Kando, Thomas M., *Leisure and Popular Culture in Transition*, Saint Louis, The C. V. Mosby Company, 1975.

Kaplan, Max, *Leisure: Theory and Policy*, New York, John Wiley and Sons, 1975.

Kidd, J. R., *How Adults Learn*, New York, Association Press, 1973.

Knowles, *The Modern Practice of Adult Education—From Pedagogy to Andragogy*, rev. ed., Chicago Association Press, Follett Publishing Company, 1980.

Knox Alan B., *Adult Development and Learning*, San Francisco, Jossey-Bass Publisher, 1977.

Kraus, Richard, *Recreation and Leisure in Modern Society*, New York, Appleton-Century-Crofts, 1971.

Kraus, Richard, *Recreation and Leisure in Modern Society*, Santa Monica, CA, Goodyear Publishing Co., 1978.

Meyer, Harold D. Meyer, Charles K. Brightbill, and H. Douglas Sessoms, *Community Recreation: A Guide to Its Organization*, 4th ed., Prentice-Hall, Inc., Englewood Cliffs, NJ, 1969.

Mundy, Jean and Linda Odum, *Leisure Education: Theory and Practice*, New York, John Wiley & Sons, 1979.

Neal, Larry (ed.), *Leisure Today: Selected Readings*, Washington, D.C., AAHPER 1975.

Neulinger, John, *The Psychology of Leisure: Research Approaches To the Study of Leisure*, Springfield, IL, Charles C Thomas, Publisher, 1974.

Neulinger, John, *To Leisure: An Introduction*, Boston, Allyn and Bacon, Inc., 1981.

Parker, J. Stanley, *The Future of Work and Leisure*, New York, Praeger Publishers, 1971.

Peters, John M., *Building an Effective Adult Education Enterprise*, San Francisco, Jossey-Bass Publishers, 1980.

Peterson, Richard E. and Associates, *Lifelong Learning in America*, San Francisco, Jossey-Bass Publishers, 1979.

Robinson, John and Geoffrey Godbey, "Work and Leisure in America: How We Spend Our Time," *Leisure Today, Journal of Physical Education and Recreation*, 49(10), 1978.

Roberts, Kenneth, *Contemporary Society and the Growth of Leisure*, New York, Longman Inc., 1978.

Shivers, Jay S., *Leisure and Recreation Concepts: A Critical Analysis*, Boston, Allyn & Bacon, Inc., 1980.

Shivers, Jay S., "Older Adulthood: New Growth Through Recreational Interaction," *Lifelong Learning: The Adult Years*, 2(1), September, 1978.

Smith, Robert M., George F. Aker, and J. R. Kidd (eds.), *Handbook of Adult Education*, New York, Macmillan Publishing Co., 1970.

Tough, Allen, *A Fresh Approach to Theory and Practice in Teaching*, San Diego, University Associates, 1980.

Tough, Allen, *Major Learning Efforts: Recent Research and Future Directions*, Ontario, Ontario Institute for Studies in Education, 1977.

Chapter II

THE IMPORTANCE OF LEISURE
IN MODERN LIVING

Tell me what you do when you are free to do as you wish, and I will tell you what kind of person you are.

Charles Brightbill
Educator

Introduction

THE PURSUIT OF HAPPINESS DURING ONE'S free hours has been described in positive terms such as relaxation, creativity, and refreshment. Ancient Greece and its golden age of cultural expansion praised leisure, the pursuit of self-enrichment and happiness and placed this concept at the center of their philosophical foundation. The pursuit of happiness has also been described in negative terms such as idleness, laziness, frivolity, or doing nothing. Many religious teachings have emphasized evil and degenerative effects arising out of indulgence in worldly pleasures. Past societies such as the Roman Empire are said to have been weakened by excessive pleasure. Regardless of the diversity of these views one fact remains unchanged, free-time pursuit of happiness has been a constant thread running through all cultural history, and it can be safely said it is a universal human phenomenon that all societies, regardless of their values, must recognize.

Today the United States' society is heavily engaged in the pursuit of happiness. Indeed it was included in our Declaration of Independence. Over one third of our waking time each week (approximately forty-eight hours) is spent in the free-time domain. As a nation we currently spend 244 billion dollars on travel, equipment, commercial entertainment, and myriad of other items that bring us pleasure.[1] If we accept the fact that the spending of money, how we allocate our scarce resources, reflects our values, then free-time pursuit of happiness is very important to this society, more important than national defense. Yet, ironically, many citizens do not rank leisure as an important part of national policy or an important part of their life-style. In times of economic stress, recreation services are one of the first to be cut by policy makers. As a nation we have no well-developed philosophy of leisure. We have no cabinet level department of leisure. The mere suggestion of such a department sounds ludicrous. United States citizens spend years of education as children preparing for the world of work, but very little of that primary and secondary education is devoted to leisure, one-third of their adult life-style. As adults, U.S. citizens willingly spend money in acquiring skills for better employment or to repair the family house and automobile. Conversely, skills in recreation or knowledge just for fun are left unattended and achieving adequate enrollment in such courses is difficult. Something needs to be said about the case for leisure and its importance in our lives. The luxury of free time and available income that our society now provides most citizens makes the pursuit of happiness possible but does not insure its success.

THE RECREATION MOVEMENT

Over the past century many social-welfare-minded leaders have recognized the right and need of all citizens to have both free time and recreational opportunities in which to pursue leisure. Jane Addams with her work at the famous Chicago Hull House promoted recreation activities for poor immigrants. By constructing one of the earliest Chicago playgrounds and establishing recreation programs for adults she encouraged healthy socialization and taught skills necessary to build a successful life in the United States.

---

[1] *U.S. News and World Report*, Aug. 10, 1981, p. 62.

The Boston sandgarden movement initiated by Maria Zak-resewska through the Massachusetts Emergency and Hygiene Association began as a playground program for poor children but was quickly expanded to programs for adults by dedicated social welfare leaders such as Joseph Lee. Lee and others saw recreation as a means to improve the quality of life for citizens living in the squalid and impoverished urban slums. Conditions in these slums, not greatly unchanged in modern ghettos, provided little opportunity for positive free-time experiences. A major cause of juvenile delinquency cases was the illegal playing of baseball in the streets. No recreation facilities were available, consequently children broke the law in their attempts to recreate. Adults suffered under the same lack of facilities, an overabundance of saloons being the only readily available alternative for recreation. Lee and his contemporaries worked to expand local government provision of recreation facilities and to expand the definition of recreation from child's play to a broad spectrum of pursuits that included young and adult alike. "Lee felt recreation had a vital significance not only for children but also for everyone who wanted a meaningful life."[2]

Since Lee's time of the early twentieth century much progress has been made in the public and private provision of recreation facilities. Television, movies, travelling, motor boating, games, spectator sports, nightclubs, are all examples of the multibillion dollar free-time recreation service system. We seem to be fulfilling the commandment of an ancient Roman emperor to give them bread and circuses in our efforts to provide more and more recreational pursuits. We have also expanded the definition of recreation to all ages from the very young to the very old. Almost everyone today feels they have a right to pursue happiness through recreation. As for the challenge of using recreation to build a meaningful life, little progress can be seen. Our high-speed, consumption-minded, work-oriented society seems more concerned on keeping people busy on the job and off the job. The development of a leisure concept and its meaning to a

---

[2]Knapp, Richard F. and Charles E. Hartsoe. *Play for America*. Arlington, VA. National Recreation and Park Association. 1979. p. 24.

personal life-style still awaits the time when we, as a nation, move beyond the point of regarding recreation as simply a "happiness pill."

The educational movement of the early twentieth century was relatively unconcerned with adult learning and the concept of leisure, focusing more attention on physical education. However, John Dewey, who promoted an educational philosophy of learning through actions and experiences, did see the great value of recreation in the childhood learning process. The 1918 Commission on Reorganization of Secondary School Education incorporated Dewey's philosophy on leisure into its seven cardinal principles of a secondary education. Cardinal principle six reads: "Worthy use of leisure: Education should equip the individual to secure from his leisure the re-creation of the body, mind and spirit, and the enrichment and enlargement of his personality."[3]

Jean Mundy has expanded and further defined this goal of leisure education. The focus of such education should be on the individual and their self-determination. Since freedom is the essence of leisure, the goal must be more than teaching correct values, attitudes, and recreation skills. Rather, greater emphasis needs to be placed on decision-making skills and the development of an ability to make personal choices. The ultimate success of leisure education is to help people learn how to achieve quality experiences in their free time.[4]

Unfortunately primary and secondary school systems have never fully embraced the task of leisure education. Milwaukee is the one notable exception where all city park and recreation services are operated by the school board. While some school systems will share land and facilities with public parks and recreation departments, it has been these latter organizations who have provided the majority of adult continuing education classes at the local level. The Mott Foundation, working through school-

[3]*Cardinal Principles of Secondary Education*, Washington, D.C., Bureau of Education, Bulletin 35, 1918, p. 14.

[4]Mundy, Jean, and Linda Odum, *Leisure Education: Theory and Practice*, New York, John Wiley and Sons, 1979, p. 244.

community organizations, has promoted similar classes through its lighted schoolhouse program, but such programs are not widespread. Art, music, and physical education are the primary free-time skills taught by our schools, and even these are suffering through budget cutbacks.

THE QUALITY OF LIFE

Many of the environmental and social factors that shaped the quality of life in the early twentieth century are still present today. The ever increasing concentration of our population into metropolitan centers brings with it mixed blessings. On one hand, population concentration makes possible larger recreation facilities and new recreation services of all varieties. Metropolitan areas are traditionally the leaders of new recreation ideas. On the other hand, population concentration places tremendous pressure on the life-style of many individuals. The degradation of growing slums, the rise in crime and social instability, the decline in air quality and other environmental conditions, and the tension of daily commuting to the suburbs are just a few of the many pressures. Many of these individuals, who for economic reasons cannot leave the city, seek temporary escape through vacation trips to parks, cottages, campgrounds, wilderness areas, and other scenic and peaceful sites. Yet for many, escape from the metropolitan life-style pressures is impossible, leaving a great need for personal adjustments, a need for placing balance in their life-style. These new workers have been completely divorced from a process of producing something tangible that was so satisfying to the early craftsmen. As a result, work is declining further in pleasure and meaning. This is unfortunate, for as long as we must work we must strive to infuse it with meaning. Our work should be what we choose to do; what we and others consider important. If leisure is to help, it must not only provide pleasure and meaning in free time, but it must also infuse our work with the same characteristics.[5] Lifting the quality of life is possible. Happier,

---

[5]Goodale, Thomas. "If Leisure is to Matter." in *Recreation and Leisure: Issues in an Era of Change.* Thomas Goodale and Peter A. Witt (eds.), State College. PA. Venture Press. 1980.

more balanced lives are possible, and leisure is one of the important keys.

Work, one's occupation, also determines the quality of life. Working well is just as important in achieving happiness as leisure. Unfortunately, the nature and meaning of work continue to change. In preindustrial periods, craftsmen derived great pleasure and meaning from the products of their labors. The nineteenth century witnessed the refinement of an assembly line technology and the inability of individual workers to build a complete product. Work declined in pleasure and meaning. Today many workers have moved beyond the factory assembly line into the area of information processing. Teachers, writers, reporters, newscasters, travel agents, and the millions of office workers are examples of occupations that involve the gathering, analysis, and communication of information.

LEISURE BENEFITS

Leisure, defined as a state of well-being, suggests that personal benefits are present. These can be conveniently grouped into six major areas: physical, social, psychological, educational, relaxational, and aesthetic. By engaging in satisfying recreation activities, an individual can ensure that personal benefits will occur in each area. Each is important, but not to the total exclusion of the others. Balance is the key to a happy life-style, and the careful selection of recreation pursuits is the key to this balance.[6] The following section will explore each of these areas and the resulting benefits.

Physiological Benefits

Participation in active recreation helps ensure physical well-being. In the past, walking and physical labor provided sufficient exercise for most people. Today, however, motorized transporta-

---

[6]Sessions, Douglas. "Lifestyles and Lifecycles: A Recreation Programming Approach." in *Recreation and Leisure: Issues in an Era of Change*, Thomas Goodale and Peter A. Witt (eds.). State College, PA, Venture Press, 1980.

tion and mechanization of labor have resulted in most people not attaining sufficient exercise in their daily routine. The dramatic rise in cardiovascular illness in recent decades can be partly attributed to lack of exercise, while being overweight, a major contribution to many health problems, is also associated with a lack of exercise.[7,8,9] One of the striking phenomena of the 1970s has been the tremendous interest in physical activities such as running, jogging, tennis, and racquet ball.[10] While commercial advertising coupled with continual medical reports on the value of exercise have certainly stimulated this interest, it is also important to note that participating in individual or dual person activities is relatively easy for adults. Team sports normally require extensive equipment and several players for a game, two conditions that are many times impossible for the individual adult. Since it is essential that physical activity be continued beyond the school years, efforts must be made to encourage lifelong recreational activities such as walking, jogging, tennis, and bicycling, all of which can be continued through the adult years.

Social Benefits

There are people we like to be with because we like them as "people." Rewarding relationships with others can occur in many contexts including marriage, family, close friendships, or casual acquaintances. At the family level a number of intimate social exchanges take place that serve to build deep affiliation. Through recreation experiences, a family finds ways to relate to each other and builds a sense of solidarity. By playing with their children, adults can establish a sense of rapport and communication that permits them to relate to their children in a meaningful manner

[7]Anderson, K. Lang, et al. *Habitual Physical Activity and Health*. Copenhagen, World Health Organization, 1978.

[8]Brunner, Daniel, "Physical Exercise and Cardiovascular Fitness," in *Guide to Fitness After Fifty*, Raymond Harris and Lawrence Frankel (eds.), New York, Plenum Press, 1978.

[9]Wilson, Philip K., *Adult Fitness and Cardiac Rehabilitation*, Baltimore, University Park Press, 1975.

[10]U.S. *News and World Report*, op.cit.

so essential to successful parenthood.[11] Families who can find time and ways to play together rarely suffer from the problems of juvenile delinquency and adolescent traumas that affect so many youth and parents.

Sports is another popular vehicle for social interaction. Engaging in sports with others provides opportunities for mutually recognizing skills, exercising leadership and self-discipline, and gaining confidence in one's ability to win or lose while still maintaining friendship. In many ways, a sporting contest is a microcosm of the great game of life with all its pressures, rewards, and disappointments, and while much has been said about the negative aspects of competition and unsportsmanlike behavior, successful participation in sports often serves to build the bond of friendship between many individuals.

Clubs, service groups, and a myriad of other social organizations serve as an expression of people's need to be with people. Here again, through free-time pursuits, an opportunity to be part of a group, to develop feelings of affiliation and *esprit de corps* is possible. Social organizations also provide the opportunity to gain new acquaintances, to establish contacts with new individuals, and to feel content in the ability to meet and establish new friendships.

Family, sports, and clubs are just three of the modes we use to seek social relationships. What is significant is the free-time atmosphere in which relaxation and personal choice make it much easier to establish bonds with those around us. One of the attractions of camping and campgrounds is the informal atmosphere where executive and janitor can sit down around the campfire and talk as persons. That temporary breakdown of class barriers and formality of our daily roles is the "social grease" of free-time and recreational pursuits that permits people to live together in harmony. The personal benefits of feeling at peace and secure with one's spouse, friends, and community and of being able to relate positively to all these individuals is extremely

---

[11]Crandall, Rick, Monica Nolan, Leslie Morgan, "Leisure and Social Interaction," in *Social Psychological Perspectives on Leisure and Recreation*, Seppo E. Iso-Ahola (ed.), Springfield, IL, Charles Thomas, Pub., 1980.

important today. Research has strongly suggested that without at least one or two intimate friends the overall health of the elderly will suffer.[12]

Relaxation Benefits

Much has been said lately about stress and well-being. In an extensive review of the subject, Kenneth Pelletur describes the increasing levels of stress in our times.

> Modern man has developed a social and economic structure and a sense of time urgency which subject him to more and greater stresses than have been experienced at any other time in human history, and the effect is often devastating. Most individuals feel that they have no choice but to accept these levels of stress as a fixed component of their Western heritage.[13]

While high levels of stress can make a life-style unpleasant, the health effects are more serious. Most standard medical textbooks attribute 50 to 80 percent of all diseases to stress-related origins. Peptic ulcers, alcoholism, cardiovascular disorders, hay fever, and hypertension are just a few of the many widespread illnesses related to stress. Hypertension alone affects an estimated 20 to 25 million people.[14]

Today's society produces stress, particularly in urban industrial areas, by bombarding us with a confusing array of smells, sounds, and people's rights. For most individuals the necessity of living in urban environments prevents escape from such stress. Eliminating the major sources of stress in one's life might mean a change in jobs, spouse, friends, and goals. Few people are sufficiently bold, free enough of commitments to others or willing to forfeit the security of a place in the system to make such changes.

Instead, many seek relief in alcohol, tranquilizers, and other socially acceptable drugs. Others simply ignore the stress and its

---

[12]Loventhal, M. F. and C. Haven. "Interaction and Adaptation: Intimacy as a Critical Variable." *American Social Review,* 33:20–30, 1968.

[13]Pelletier, Kenneth R. *Mind As Healer, Mind As Slayer.* New York, Delta Publishing Co., 1977, p. 3.

[14]Ibid. p. 7.

effects. However, a growing number are turning to recreation as a primary mode for stress reduction and relaxation. Some people find relaxation through physical activities such as sports, jogging, or gardening. For others the intense mental activity of playing chess or bridge, working a crossword puzzle, or reading a difficult novel brings relaxation. Still others find relaxation not through physical or mental activity but from an absence of it, daydreaming, dozing, or possibly watching TV. All these relaxational activities involve some element of escape; while this does not solve problems, it certainly provides needed relief and refreshment.[15]

Due to continual increases of complexity and overstimulation in modern society, a counter movement has begun to control stress while promoting relaxation and health. This movement is termed life-styling, a conscious determination on the part of the individual to control the conditions of a personal living environment in a manner that will maximize personal development of body, mind, and spirit.[16] This holistic concept is analogous to the concept of leisure as a state of well-being, and many life-styling techniques rely on good use of free time through appropriate recreational activities.

Educational Benefits

It has been traditional to think of adult education as serving a vocational purpose, indeed many of the programs and courses do. However, there are many nonvocational adult education programs especially in the arts, humanities, social sciences, and recreational skills. Here, much of the motivation for participation and the benefits derived come from the intrinsic enjoyment of acquiring new knowledge. "Informal teaching methods, extensive class participation and lengthy discussion periods are typical features of adult courses. They are studied and taught for their general relatedness to life, for generalized reflection and discussion,

---

[15]Chubb, Michael and Holly Chubb. *One Third of Our Time*. New York, John Wiley and Sons, 1981

[16]Pelletier, op. cit.

and above all for their personal relevance."[17] For many adults, the content knowledge gained from a course is extrinsic to their main purpose for participating—fun.

Motivation for adult leisure learning takes two major forms, a desire to understand and a desire to create. Beginning with a desire to understand and proceeding at their own pace, many adults will move from the realm of learning into the realm of action by creating new experiences that enhance their life-styles. Folk art and crafts are a popular example. Religious study is another. Many modes exist. Some adults read history and then plan trips to visit historical sites. At times it is difficult to distinguish the works of the serious amateur from those of the professional, but what distinguishes the two groups is the motivation behind the activity. What distinguishes the amateur philosopher, novelist, poet, or scientist is that his preoccupation may persist over time and end in contribution but it *need* not."[18]

A number of recreational activities result in learning. Antique collectors, for example, often become fascinated by the history of past eras and seek through reading and travel to historic sites to understand more of the tools and furnishings that our forefathers used. Likewise rock collectors learn geology, bird watchers become knowledgeable about nature, and photographers find out about physics of light. Travel can be highly educational as well as recreational especially when it involves exploration of new cultures and new environments here and abroad. Pursuing all these activities and many more is fun; in this case, fun can be educational.

Raghib and Beard divided the educational component of leisure satisfaction into four parts: learning about things around oneself, learning about oneself, learning about other people, and learning about opportunities to try new things.[19] The types of satisfactions derived from each of these categories can be multifaceted. For example, learning about things around oneself

[17]Godbey, Geoffrey and Stanley Parker. *Leisure Studies and Services: An Overview.* Philadelphia, W. B. Saunders, 1976, pp. 48–9.

[18]Kaplan, Max. *Leisure: Lifestyle and Lifespan.* Philadelphia, W. B. Saunders, 1979, p. 158.

[19]Raghib, M. G. and J. G. Beard, "Leisure Satisfaction: Concept, Theory, and Measurement" in *Social Psychological Perspectives on Leisure and Recreation.* Seppo E. Iso-Ahola (ed.), Springfield, IL, Charles Thomas, Pub., 1980.

adds a sense of variety and personal achievement to a life-style. Becoming an expert on a particular topic provides a chance to exhibit one's achievement and brings compliments from others. On the other hand, learning about oneself can develop a profound sense of independence, self-esteem, and self-responsibility. In the words of Aristotle "a life unexamined is not worth living."

Great satisfaction can also come from learning about others. Witness the abundance of adult encounter groups that promote greater understanding and tolerance of our fellow human beings. Many adults strive to know others better not only to derive satisfaction from their company but also in order to avoid undue stress or rejection.

Finally, learning of opportunities for recreation participation can greatly enhance a life-style. Many adults fall into lifetime routines called "recreation ruts" that change little after the early years of youth and school. Simply knowing of new opportunities can give sufficient impetus to attempt a new activity that may open the door to a whole new world of pleasure.

Psychological Benefits

Sebastian De Grazia, a noted social critic and author of the book Of Time, Work and Leisure, often proclaims, and rightly so, that freedom is the essence of leisure.[20] Leisure is synonymous with individual freedom, the license to try new experiences, to face new challenges. All of us derive great benefit from experimenting with our free time, exploring new recreational activities. Sampling from a wide range of activities adds variety to one's life-style and satisfaction that they have followed their dreams and wishes.

In a nation of over 225 million people, bombarded by a media that makes heroes for only a small select number, all individuals have a need for some form of status and recognition. Pursuit of recreation activities offers many opportunities for achievement of status and recognition. The hobbiest who exhibits great skill and

---

[20]De Grazia, Sebastian, Of Time, Work and Leisure, Garden City, N.J. Doubleday—Anchor, 1962.

knowledge in growing roses or a vegetable garden often is recognized as a local expert. How often has one listened to a world traveler and seen the status he/she achieves through recounting visits to many foreign lands. Other individuals achieve recognition and status through outstanding community service. The range of recreation activities is great, and there are opportunities where each individual can be recognized for their great skill and knowledge.

Another important psychological benefit derived through recreation involves dominance and the ability to influence others in one's own social environment. The need for dominance is particularly strong today due to our working conditions and the increasing number of social regulations. To balance the requirements of obeying one's boss, of obeying the laws, etc., many individuals seek out recreational activities that put them in charge. For example, a president of a local club or organization can exercise a tremendous amount of leadership and influence. Here are opportunities to influence not only one's peers but also one's local environment through organizational effort. Others seek control of their immediate environment by escaping to a weekend cottage or the outdoors. In such semi-isolated places one has more freedom to do as one pleases. Other individuals with extremely high dominance needs can be seen conquering mountains and pitting themselves against the dangers of wild rivers. However, leadership and dominance need not be dangerous or linked to organized activity. Recreation offers many avenues of opportunity where individuals may take charge of their free time and desires, leading themselves in self-directed activity.

While freedom, recognition, and dominance are important psychological benefits, we need, above all, a sense of enjoyment and accomplishment in our lives. Alexander Reid-Martin, a well-known psychiatrist, who served for twelve years as chairman of the American Psychiatric Association's Committee on Leisure Time and Its Uses, has written extensively on the importance of exercising one's personal skills and abilities. Reid-Martin states that each person has what he terms an innate capacity to act. Responding to these inner urges brings great personal satisfactions.[21] Others have described these inner urges in terms of creativity or self-actualization. Regardless of the term, recreation activities coupled with the concept of free choice provides abundant opportunities to act, to be, in a manner that is pleasing to one's self. In an increasingly crowded world where personal choices to act are becoming increasingly limited, recreation is one of the last frontiers where one can choose to pursue activities of one's interest.

Many times the psychological benefits of leisure are taken for granted and accorded little importance. This is an unfortunate attitude since healthy recreational pursuits are so very important to mental health. Sometimes this importance can only be recognized during periods of psychological or emotional stress. "Then individuals, or their friends and relatives, may recognize their mental health is endangered and that participation in a recreation activity is likely to be of assistance."[22]

These authors go on to point out numerous ways people use recreation to restore emotional balance:

> Individuals who have recently moved or been bereaved or divorced join social or hobby clubs to make new friends and dispel chronic loneliness. A person who is going through some type of personal crisis seeks comfort and peace in aesthetic experiences such as watching a sunset, viewing a work of art, reading a poem, or listening to soothing music. An introverted individual acquires a knowledge of certain recreation activities to use as a source of topics for conversation and to help build self-confidence and gain acceptance in social situations. People who feel obliged to repress their emotions at work or in their personal relationships find harmless outlets for their aggressive feelings by watching contact sports on television, by facing and meeting the challenges inherent in high-risk activities, by participating vigorously in sports, or by engaging in a variety of simple activities like kicking a ball around a backyard, going for a ride on a bicycle or motorcycle, or shooting at a target. Isolated, lonely individuals keep their television sets turned on all day long, since the people in the television programs provide a link to the outside world and serve as surrogate companions.[23]

---

[21]Reid-Martin, Alexander. "Leisure and Our Inner Resources." *Parks and Recreation.* 3:1–16. 1975.

[22]Chubb, Michael, and Holly Chubb. *One Third of Our Time.* New York, John Wiley and Sons. 1981. p. 56.

[23]Ibid.

In summary, there are many psychological benefits of a satisfying leisure state. Many of our life's efforts are directed to this end although, strangely enough, most individuals are unaware of leisure's importance to their life-style.

Aesthetic Benefits

Aesthetic recreation are those feelings that arise from an appreciation of beauty as opposed to utility or usefulness. All individuals have experienced the deep emotional feelings and sensations that are evoked by the belle arts: music, drama, and dance. These performing arts have been appreciated by generations for the great pleasure given by their beauty and grace. Paintings, pottery, sculptures, or work crafted by other artisians hold great attraction. Mother nature herself offers a rich opportunity for aesthetic appreciation. Sitting on a cliff watching a brilliant sunset or discovering a new flower in the spring woods can bring forth feelings of awe and affection for the natural world.

One of the greatest benefits of free time is the opportunity to pursue recreation activities that lead to aesthetic experiences. Indeed, the word recreation implies an uplifting of the spirit, a re-creation, and it is unfortunate that so often the term is restricted in meaning to simple physical restoration. For many, pursuit of aesthetic experiences requires active participation, but for others emotional participation is sufficient. Regardless of the mode of participation, the range of recreational activities offers a tremendous selection of settings within which one can achieve aesthetic experiences.

While the value of aesthetic experiences is great, there is a broader, perhaps more important, benefit that springs from leisure, that of religious celebration. Many holidays have religious celebration as their justification and even our most basic rhythm of work and rest is based on religious doctrine, six days of work and one day of rest. Alexander Reid-Martin points out quite well the important relationship between leisure and religion.

> The religions of the world, implicitly and explicitly, have stressed the need for leisure. Many have regarded the biblical phrase "waiting on the Lord" as an exhortation to be still, to let be, to relax and surrender

ourselves to leisure, to contemplate, meditate, wonder, and marvel. The last chapter of the 13th verse [sic] of Isaiah says it all: "They that wait upon the Lord shall renew their strength, they shall mount up with wings of eagles, they shall run and not be weary, they shall walk and not faint."

The revered religions of the East, particular Buddhism, place their greatest emphasis upon mental and/or physical relaxation and its indispensability for healthy growth.[24]

Rest and relaxation are important prerequisites to worship and all religions recognize this as evidenced by their rituals and customs. Joseph Peiper, an eminent theologian and philosopher, sees the culmination of these rituals and customs in a religious celebration from which mankind "may truly be 'transported' out of the weariness of daily labor into an unending holiday, carried away out of the straightners of the work a day world into the heart of the universe."[25] Such an aesthetic experience comes from the affirmation of deep personal values and a feeling that one is able to act in response to those values despite outside pressures to do otherwise. The personal benefits of this experience hardly need enumeration. For many, religious experiences are a powerful determinant in their lives, and leisure is intimately connected with these experiences.

SUMMARY

Phi Delta Kappa[26] published a list of eighteen educational goals which has been adopted by Verduin to a list of 16 goals for adult education.[27] Leisure, the ability to use free time productively, appears in both lists but is consistently ranked low in importance by most adult educators. Why is this so? Perhaps it is due to a popular view of leisure as a series of trivial, funlike activities. Certainly that view of leisure, when compared to goals

---

[24]Reid-Martin, Alexander. "Leisure and Our Inner Resources". *Parks and Recreation*. 3:3, 1975.

[25]Peiper, Joseph, *Leisure, The Basis of Culture*, New York, Pantheon, 1952, p. 64.

[26]For a discussion of the goals, see Harold Spears, "Kappans Ponder the Goals of Education." *Phi Delta Kappa*, 55 (1):29–32, 1973.

[27]Verduin, John R., Jr., *Curriculum Building for Adult Learning*, Carbondale, IL, Southern Illinois University Press, 1980, pp. 61–62.

such as reading, writing, healthy social relationships, and occupational training deserves a low ranking. Hopefully, this chapter has
shown that leisure is much more than trivial fun-time activities.

Leisure is living one's life to the fullest, and this concept
encompasses all of the goals on those two lists. Through personal choice and good use of free time, many of those educational goals can be achieved. Education can be fun. Free time,
which occupies over one third of the average person's waking
hours, can be fun and also educational. Both occupy a significant
part of our life-style, and both contribute to a state of leisure
well-being.

Like the "Fiddler on the Roof" we all strive somehow to keep a
sense of balance in our lives. Leisure is one very important
balancing factor. The requirements of work, food, sleep, home
repairs, and other necessities place a number of relatively unnego-
tiable demands upon the individual that can serve to unbalance
a life-style. The tension or drudgery associated with completing
required tasks leaves one exhausted and many times unsatisfied.
Leisure, through appropriate selection of recreational activities
can help restore a zest to life. Leisure offers the counterbalance.
Highly stressful jobs can be compensated by the selection of
relaxing recreation; unimaginative, boring jobs can be compensated for by the selection of exciting, stressful recreation. Whatever the personal need, if it is not being met in the work arena, it
can be found in the leisure arena.

Moreover, each individual has the opportunity and the responsibility to make good choices of recreational activities and to
judge the success of that activity by his/her own standards. Each of
us, in our own way, is a free-time manager responsible for arranging recreational activities that best meet our own needs. The
standards of success or failure in this task are very individualistic.
Are we making ourselves happy? Are we living life according to
our needs and wishes? Are we achieving a state of leisure well-
being? These are questions each must answer alone. They are
important questions and so is leisure. It is one of the most
important parts of our modern lives.

SELECTED BIBLIOGRAPHY

Anderson, K. Lange, et. al., Habitual Physical Activity and Health, Copenhagen, World Health Organization, 1978.

Ardell, Donald P., High Level Wellness—An Alternative to Doctors, Drugs, and Disease, Emmaus, PA, Rodale Press, 1977.

Bammel, Gene and Lu Lane Burrus-Bammel, Leisure and Human Behavior, Dubuque, IA, Wm. C. Brown, 1982.

Brummer, Daniel, "Physical Exercise and Cardiovascular Fitness," in Guide to Fitness After Fifty, Raymond Harris and Lawrence Frankel (eds.), New York, Plenum Press, 1978.

Carlson, Reynold Edgar, Janet R. MacLean, Theodore R. Deppe, and James A. Peterson, Recreation and Leisure, The Changing Scene, 3rd ed., Belmont, California, Wadsworth, 1979.

Chubb, Michael and Holly Chubb, One Third of Our Time? An Introduction to Recreation Behavior and Resources, New York, John Wiley and Sons, 1981.

De Grazia, Sebastian, Of Time, Work and Leisure, New York, Twentieth Century Fund, 1962.

Ellis, M. J., Why People Play, Englewood Cliffs, New Jersey, Prentice-Hall, 1973.

Godbey, Geoffrey and Stanley Parker, Leisure Studies and Services: An Overview, Philadelphia, W. B. Saunders Company, 1976.

Godbey, Geoffrey, Leisure in Your Life: An Exploration, Philadelphia, Saunders College Publishing, 1981.

Goodale, Thomas L. and Peter A. Witt (eds.), Recreation and Leisure: Issues in an Era of Change, State College, Pennsylvania, Venture Publishing, 1980.

Haworth, J. T. and M. A. Smith, Work and Leisure, Princeton, New Jersey, Princeton Book Company, 1976.

Iso-Ahola, Seppo E. (ed.), Social Psychological Perspectives on Leisure and Recreation, Springfield, Illinois, Charles C Thomas, Publisher, 1980.

Iso-Ahola, Seppo E., The Social Psychology of Leisure and Recreation, Debuque, IA, Wm. C. Brown Company, Publishers, 1980.

Kando, Thomas M., Leisure and Popular Culture in Transition, St. Louis, C. V. Mosby Company, 1975.

Kaplan, Max, Leisure: Lifestyle and Lifespan Perspectives for Gerontology, Philadelphia, W. B. Saunders, 1979.

Kaplan, Max, Leisure: Theory and Policy, New York, John Wiley and Sons, 1975.

Kelley, John R., Leisure, Englewood Cliffs, New Jersey, Prentice-Hall, 1982.

Kraus, Richard, Recreation and Leisure in Modern Society, 2nd ed., Santa Monica, CA, Goodyear, 1978.

Knapp, Richard A. and Charles E. Hartsoe, Play For America, The National Recreation Association 1906–1965, Arlington, VA, National Recreation and Park Association, 1979.

Levy, Joseph, Play Behavior, New York, John Wiley and Sons, 1978.

Mundy, Jean and Linda Odum, Leisure Education: Theory and Practice, New York, John Wiley and Sons, 1979.

Neulinger, John, *The Psychology of Leisure*, Springfield, IL, Charles C Thomas, Publisher, 1974.

Neulinger, John, *To Leisure: An Introduction*, Boston, Allyn and Bacon, Inc., 1981.

Pelletin, Kenneth, *Mind is Healer, Mind is Slayer*, New York, Delta, 1977.

Pelletin, Kenneth, *Holistic Health: From Stress to Optimum Health*, New York, Delacorte, 1979.

Rapoport, Rhona and Robert Rapoport, *Leisure and the Family Life Cycle*, Boston, Routledge and Kegan, 1975.

Reid-Martin, Alexander, "Leisure and Our Inner Resources," *Parks and Recreation*, 10(3):1–16, 1976.

Shivers, Jay S., *Leisure and Recreation Concepts: A Critical Analysis*, Boston, Allyn and Bacon Inc., 1981.

Wilson, Philip K., *Adult Fitness and Cardiac Rehabilitation*, Baltimore, University Park Press, 1975.

Chapter **III**

ADULT CHARACTERISTICS AND LEISURE LEARNING

Introduction

A N ADULT IS AS COMPLEX AND every bit as much of an individual as his counterpart, the public-school-age individual. We speak of and pay attention to the individual differences of children and youth when thinking about and designing learning experiences for them. We also know that children and youth go through a variety of developmental stages as they move toward adulthood. The very same thing can be said for adults as they move from the young adult years to those of the postretirement or senior-citizen years.

Adults are different from one another because of their socialization process and their biological dimensions. The numerous experiences that they have had while living on this earth have caused them to differ if ever so slightly, and these differences are not attributable to age, but to differences in the experiences, sociocultural backgrounds, and educational attainments of adults. Experiencing within the socialization process has caused definite behaviors (personalities) to be formed on the part of each adult. Each adult possesses certain beliefs, attitudes, needs, values, and self-experiences that formulate a perceptual package that governs the behavior pattern of the adult. Different needs, values and beliefs can cause adults to see things differently as they move throughout life; thus the importance of these in terms of individual differences can be seen. These perceptual packages and resulting behaviors affect how an adult responds to free time use

37

and leisure learning; in turn, participation in recreation modifies perceptual packages. For instance, adults have generally learned about 50 percent of their leisure activities as youngsters because of their families and friends (their individual subculture) and their influences. This earlier socialization process has had an impact on adults and their total leisure behavior.

Biological differences among adults have also had an impact upon their leisure interests and uses. Physical limitations can preclude participation in certain leisure and recreational activities. However, some good physical abilities can encourage other adults to engage in numerous activities as they seek to enhance the quality of their lives through leisure activities.

Developmental stages can be identified within adult life that can cause adults to respond differently to leisure use and learning than they may have previously. These cycles are generally experienced by all adults as changes occur in the roles they play and the crises they experience. Life is not an easy transition from young adulthood to senior adulthood. Problems, concerns, and developments impact on the adult and his/her leisure use and participation. Although adult developmental stages, much as in children, are not precise, some apparent patterns are quite discernible as the adult moves through life. This chapter will take a brief look at adult development stages in three major categories—the younger adult, the middle-aged adult, and the older adult—and then seek some implications for leisure learning programming and use.

THE YOUNGER ADULT

The younger adult stage begins with the breaking of psychological ties as one moves from the "nest" to take off on one's own life pattern. This could include looking for a job, choosing a career, or attending school. This early stage includes handling one's own time, adjusting to one's life on his/her own, and managing the stress of the accompanying change. At this point, young adults generally have full physical abilities; thus physical recreation is very popular for this group, especially among the unmarried. Class status, as throughout much of adult life, will have an effect on leisure activities. Those from more affluent backgrounds may engage more in formal clubs, groups, and organizations. Also, the nature of one's employment can cause different recreation patterns.

Besides the breaking away from home and the movement into some employment opportunities, the selection of a mate can have a major effect on the younger adult; getting married will change the patterns of leisure use. As the unmarried enjoyed social contacts, the newly formed couple will seek other contacts. Couples will attempt to seek recreation activities that can be shared by both. If this is not the case, some tension can occur among young marrieds. If both of the young marrieds are working, some complications may arise in terms of the use of the extra money. Buying or saving money for a house may impact on the use of money for recreation. If a couple opts for less lofty home living, more money may be available for leisure use: the opposite can, of course, cause less leisure-use expenditures. The young married couple may still maintain their previous leisure contacts and engage in numerous physical activities, but this will begin to wane.

The advent of parenthood also reduces the range of recreation activities especially among the mothers. With parenthood the availability of time and money can become a problem and will generally lead to more changes in recreation patterns; children increase obligations for the parents that add to the existence and subsistence needs of the family and not recreation activities.

Perhaps the greatest change in free-time use after parenthood is toward a family and home orientation. Doing things as a family and around the home is prevalent at this time with much less interaction with peer groups apparent. After parenthood some adult associations can occur in sports and recreation with encouragement by spouses, but males appear to participate more than females. However, the changes in the woman's role in society may increase recreation activity. This remains to be seen. In essence few new recreation interests are acquired after marriage with the exception of home projects. Home-centered activities are big at this time, and, as will be noted later, after retirement. Thus, at this stage, family and careers can constrain recreation activities in a number of ways and can reduce many associations. However, it might be noted that despite work and family obligations some better planning does exist and organizing time for better leisure use is very possible.

THE MIDDLE-AGED ADULT

As the adult moves toward the middle-age years of life, problems and crises will arise that can impact on the life-style of the individual. Marital difficulties and the reassessment of the marriage itself can occur. Occupational frustrations and the reexamination of the work activity can come forth. A real reevaluation of personal priorities, goals, and values and the entire life-style of an adult can take place during this period of life. This entire midlife reexamination and the accompanying midlife crises do impact heavily on adults.

Family changes such as children leaving home and the concern for aging parents as well as the diminishing of physical abilities further contribute to the midlife assessment.

With apparently more time available because of less immediate family responsibilities and the loss of child-centered and child-determined schedules, adults at this age level will begin to increase social activities. Also, family and work changes may cause people to engage in new kinds of athletic and cultural activities. However, strenuous sports and physically demanding outdoor recreational activities decrease not only because of physical limitations but also because of role expectations. Social pressures can cause rather stable positions and some settling in and acceptance of oneself does occur. Some passive and familiar recreation routines seem to prevail.

With domestic responsibilities decreased more recreation should be expected, but little increase in participation recreation takes place. There may be some increase in community-based activities such as church and civic organizations but this is not typical. More interaction with old acquaintances and the establishment of new ones seem to prevail. It appears that recreation activities and interests become increasingly restricted with age despite decreased responsibilities. The social class of the adult still has an impact at this age, with those of lower status spending recreation opportunities with the extended family and around the house, and the more affluent are more involved in groups and voluntary organizations. Unfortunately, less recreation activity does seem to prevail, probably because of a decline in mental and physical vigor and because the recreation industries are geared for the younger adult. In the latter case it is strongly implied that fun and games are for the young, not the old.

As the adult moves through the middle-age stage to the later years of life, the social cycle shrinks and an active social life decreases. Also, the separation from a mate through death or divorce can have a heavy impact on recreation activities. Grief, suffering, and possible financial problems can result from the separation even though perceived increased freedom may be present. And, the loss of a mate with whom to do things can cause loneliness.

THE OLDER ADULT

As the adult approaches the latter years of life, numerous other problems can come into being that will affect leisure and leisure use. Besides the potential advent of widowhood, the elderly adult will generally retire from work, experience problems, have possible financial problems, and even have questions of personal worth. All of these factors can and will have an impact on the life-style of the older adult. American adults are living longer now than ever before basically because of medical science and social welfare efforts. Thus, more elderly adults are present, and these adults have a definite need for leisure experiences.

The advent of widowhood can cause a major problem, especially if there was a close, intimate relationship. The loss requires a new orientation to leisure because the adult may be left out of social activities that were couple oriented. The adult must seek out others in similar situations and/or seek out noncouple activities. More nonfamilial and independent behaviors have to be developed. Not only the loss of a mate but the loss of other family members and friends have an effect on leisure behavior. These losses leave a void in the adult's social system that must be replaced for continued effective living.

The process of retiring from one's occupational endeavors too can place a definite strain on the adult and related recreation practices. The difficulty can come from the loss of associations, life patterns, and physical surroundings. The problem may be greater for men because the sharp 8 to 5 routine is broken; it may be somewhat easier for women on less defined schedules. Working-class men and women can have more problems than the middle- and upper-class people. The latter group can get into volunteer work and other activities much easier. "Workaholics" can experience great difficulty with leisure experiences after retirement as well as those people with a poor history of leisure satisfaction. Even though more time is available after retirement, a feeling of meaninglessness, despair, and obsolescence can affect the retiree, and adequate recreation experiences can be important here. Restructuring a routine, other than a Monday through Friday one, is a major transitional task.

Health problems can also impact on the recreation participation by older adults. Chronic illnesses such as arthritis and diabetes or having problems with one's heart, eyes, hearing, or other physical areas can limit mobility and active physical participation in many instances. This is when recreation participation declines most in those activities outside the home and those that require physical exertion. Such things as sewing, handicrafts, working in the garden, woodworking and extensive travel may be replaced by watching television, reading, and having discussions and chats with other adults. These substitutions of activity can result in very positive experiences that can still enhance the quality of life for adults. In many cases, very limited resources are available to elderly adults who live on a fixed income in later years. Limited income can preclude extensive travel, membership in various organizations, attendance at various functions that require admission fees, and other recreation activities where some cost may be involved.

All of the above-mentioned factors can lead elderly adults to question their very self-worth. After an active life at work, raising a family, and other forms of vigorous, healthy activity, the adult can be left with a feeling of "what's the use;" continued withdrawal from recreational and social participation can occur. Personal reasons for the withdrawal or disengagement from activities and groups can come from a feeling of little self-worth or despair and stagnation.

Even though numerous problems do confront the elderly in terms of recreational pursuits, the additional free time can be put to good use. For those who have good health and sufficient finances, travel and numerous other activities can be pursued. Older people generally wish to be active and need and enjoy socializing. Social participation, face-to-face interaction, is very big for these adults and even exceeds television and listening to the radio in terms of interest and desire. It is felt that adults could, of course, do more if cost, mobility, and safety were considered.

Older adults again have many home-centered activities, but seldom take up totally new recreation activities. Some changes in activities do occur but generally within the existing recreation repertoire. If, for example, adults have played cards quite a bit in earlier years, they may engage in new card games or board games, but probably won't take off in an entirely new direction or activity. The extra time that the older adults have for leisure is generally used to do many of the same things that were done before only they do them more slowly. It appears that the activity is expanded to make it fit into the additional time available; similar tasks, activities and relationships may expand to fill the new time. For example, if a woman played bridge once a month with her friends, she is likely to play once a week presently. Or if the man went fishing once a week, he may fish every day or every other day after retirement. There is definitely more time to do things previously done, and there is more freedom to do them in depth.

If finances are available the elderly adult may secure new equipment for leisure use. The adult may purchase a more sophisticated camera and trade in the older one, or secure a new lathe or saw, or purchase a more modern sewing machine all of which can be used for leisure activities. But again significant changes in recreation experiences simply do not occur for the elderly, and only some changes within larger patterns are witnessed.

SOME GENERALIZATIONS

From reviewing the evidence on recreational activity and the life stages of adults, it is clearly shown that the older the individual is the lower the level of general activity. From their investigation Gordon, Gaitz, and Scott found that "the negative relationship between life cycle stage and leisure participation is dramatic: respondents in the youngest group (20–29) are almost four times as likely to report high levels of leisure participation (80+ percent) than are those in the oldest group (75 years and over, approximately 24 percent). Both males and females show similar strong negative associations between life-stage and leisure participation."[1] The lower frequency of participation for those with increasing age came in activities that are generally done outside the home and that involved a good degree of physical exertion, excitement, and escape and some high intensity of involvement such as dancing, outdoor activities, sports, and traveling.

Some recreational activities seem to hold fairly equal over the life span of the adult. Such activities as TV viewing, spectator sports, club membership, and home embellishment appear to be quite constant as the adult moves throughout life. These activities, of course, are more sedentary in nature and require lower levels of intense involvement, and many can be done in the home. Thus, outside-the-home, intense, physical activities will decline substantially with age, but moderately intense and home-based activities, particularly socialization, remain about equal in terms of participation.

Two leisure categories as reported by Gordon, Gaitz, and Scott actually showed an increase with the aging process, cooking (by men only) and relaxation/solitary.[2] These increases probably reflect the opportunity for fewer social contacts for older people and less available money and other resources. Relaxation and solitude were deemed more important in each successive age group.

---

[1]Gordon, Chad, Charles M. Gaitz, and Judith Scott, "Leisure and Lives: Personal Expressivity Across the Life Span," in *Handbook of Aging and the Social Sciences*, R. H. Binstock and E. Shanas (eds.), New York, Van Nostrand-Reinhold Co., 1976, p. 326.

[2]Ibid.

Some male–female bifurcation is apparent throughout the life span of adults. Men tend to be more high-intensity and externally oriented in recreational activities, while women tend to spend more free time in television viewing, relaxation and solitude, cooking, and home embellishment, which are more internal and less intense in nature. Social roles appear to have an affect here. In terms of leisure, the pleasure experienced appears to be little different between the sexes at any age level. Men derived pleasure from their activities and women from theirs.

Thus, it appears that recreational use generally decreases over the life span of an adult. From greater and more intense activity at the early stages the adult moves throughout life in search of recreational opportunities that are less intense, more sedate, and more passive in nature. The adult also moves from external to internal and even individual activities during free time use. Relaxation and solitude and home-based activities are very popular for the elderly adult where at the other end of the continuum, the young adult engages in more intense and greater physical activity. And, little changes within existing general patterns of recreational activities are apparent.

IMPLICATIONS FOR LEISURE LEARNING

From this brief overview of life stages and corresponding free-time use, some ideas might be advanced for consideration by adult education leisure specialists as they help the adult in successful aging and successful free-time use. The ultimate goal for these specialists is to help adults achieve a leisure state of mind, a state of well-being, a feeling good about one's life, actually developing a good mental health status. Effective free-time use and recreational activities are important to successful aging and a state of well-being if continued throughout the life span of people. As Iso-Ahola offers, "continued participation in recreational activities throughout the entire life cycle is characteristic of those who live long and age successfully. It is important to note that involvement in all three types of activities (motor, cognitive, and affective) was positively related to mental health. One implication of this result is that a variety of activities is needed for successful aging, and that those who follow this pattern are psychologically healthy. This reflects the importance of having opportunities to seek novelty through a variety of activities."[3] It is interesting to note that cognitive activities ranked highly in terms of physical health when considering recreational engagement. Significant thought processes as well as motor activity lead to the notion that active participation in a variety of recreational activities is important.

As the adult education leisure specialist moves toward some action in programming recreational experiences to assist adults achieve a leisure state of mind, the nature of the population to be served must be an initial concern. Sessoms points this out candidly by suggesting that "the first step necessary in the implementation of this action is the recognition of the target groups to be served. Different lifestyles and different life stages require different programs and program approaches."[4] A knowledge and understanding of the adult clients, their interests and needs, their learning styles, their previous experiences, their successes and failures, and their total lifestyles will, of course, lead to a variety of different strategies since adults simply are different from one another. Some adults may require carefully supervised activities, while others would like greater freedom. Some may wish more structured and formal learning experiences, while some may wish to have a totally self-directed experience. Perhaps the biggest factor in designing experiences for adults is determining their interests, needs, and backgrounds at various stages in their lives. Thus, a corollary to this first point relates to determining exactly what are the needs and interests of the adult clients.

A needs assessment or inventory can provide the data to help determine the desires of adults for additional learning, and also the kinds of programming of experiences that will help accomplish this learning. With this information the leisure education

[3]Iso-Ahola, Seppo E., *The Social Psychology of Leisure and Recreation*. Dubuque. Iowa. Wm. C. Brown Company Publishers, 1980. p. 178.

[4]Sessoms. H. Douglas. "Lifestyles and Lifecycles: A Recreation Programming Approach." in *Recreation and Leisure: Issues in an Era of Change*, Thomas L. Goodale and Peter A. Witt (eds.), State College. PA. Venture Publishing Co., 1980. p. 194.

specialist can begin to design required experiences based on available space, resources, and people. Without information on the adult clients and their total package of needs, interests, and concerns, recreational programming will become fruitless quickly.

The securing of appropriate space, resources, and people has implications for programming of learning experiences too. To carry on effective lifelong learning for adults, consideration must be given to the location of experiences and accessibility, the cost, the timing, the various materials used, the nature of the instruction, the instructor, if used, and procedural concerns. If these are not considered carefully, they can rapidly become barriers to the continued learning of adults.[5]

Another concern or implication for successful programming of leisure learning experiences for adults would fall in the category of informing the adult clients about the numerous opportunities and services available. As Sessoms suggests, this "involves the amassing and dissemination of information and knowledge about activities and services offered. This approach embraces the concepts of leisure counseling and leisure consulting, including the offering of technical assistance."[6] The flow of information should not only indicate what activities are available, but what can become available and what is possible, as well as what benefits can be derived from active participation. This then will raise the level of awareness of the adults in terms of the total leisure education concept. Adults can not act on an experience until some awareness has been achieved. Adults lack total awareness of the many possibilities and benefits that can be derived from lifelong learning experiences. With a more effective communication process in action perhaps greater activity in recreational activities can occur. The opposite effect of poor communication can definitely cause a barrier to lifelong learning.

Sessoms, again in his essay, suggests that a major thrust in any program for leisure use should focus on learning.[7] This, of

---

[5]Peterson, Richard E. and Associates, *Lifelong Learning in America*, San Francisco, Jossey-Bass Publishers, 1979.

[6]Sessoms, op. cit. p. 194.

[7]Sessoms, op. cit.

course, is important for those adults who wish to learn new skills and ideas in recreation, but it is more important for all adults who want to become knowledgeable about free-time use and the qualities of well-being and effective living. At any life stage and within any life-style, the adult can learn not only specifics but how to develop a better state of being.

To assist in adult learning, adult education leisure specialists must have full comprehension of life stages of adults, their life-styles and their behaviors. These specialists must be aware of the motivations and life roles that their adult clients possess at the time of programming and the total behavioral package that adult clients possess. As suggested earlier the adult is very much an individual. Learning among all adults is very much an individual effort. Adults vary greatly in their abilities and disabilities related to learning and adult education leisure specialists must emphasize the abilities of adults and minimize the disabilities as they help their clients move toward a better state of being.

Adult learners definitely have different rates of learning which obviously would argue for a self-pacing strategy in the programming of learning experiences for adults. However, it should be kept in mind that adults, in contrast to children, have had many experiences, and those professionals involved must keep this in mind and draw upon these many experiences as they design learning activities.

Adults like things of interest to them and also find great interest in hands-on type of learning experiences. Adults also can learn from a variety of learning experiences, not just one set method. Adults too like to know how they are doing during learning activities (feedback), and they don't want to waste their time. These have definite implications for the work of the adult leisure specialist.

Adults can have some deterioration in problem-solving abilities, and a short-term memory decline is very possible. Also physical problems such as seeing and hearing can impact on the adult's learning ability.

As suggested above, there are numerous individual differences among adults, but they are not generally related to age; other subcultural factors are involved here. It is suggested that those with recent educational experiences tend to do better than those who have not had them.

Probably the key to assisting adults in their leisure learning experiences is to set realistic goals, provide a challenge to them, and let them pursue their learning experiences with freedom at their speed. Again, self-pacing learning experiences have been most effective for adult learners.

As mentioned in Chapter I, considerable learning by adults is done in a self-directed and self-conducted manner. Adults, being continuous learners, are confronted with tasks and concerns almost constantly that they wish to explore, learn more about, and perhaps solve. They set out on their own, or sometimes with a friend or peer, to gain new information and skills and work at their own pace.

Adults engage in this form of self-directed learning for a number of reasons. According to Penland the major reasons are a desire to set one's own pace, to put one's own structure on the learning project, to use one's own style of learning, to keep the learning strategy flexible and open to change, and to learn about it right away and not wait until some sort of class may begin. The lack of time for and the dislike of a formal class situation and, quite surprisingly, cost of and transportation to formal classes were ranked lowest by respondents as reasons for engaging in self-directed learning.[8] High among the learning projects in which adults engage using this methodology are recreational (hobbies) and self-enrichment activities. Thus, adult leisure specialists should be aware of this.

The specialist can provide assistance to the self-directed learning process of adults with the development of all kinds of information and materials for use. Further, the specialist can help adults with strategies for self-directed learning in recreational areas. Assistance is needed in helping adults know how to start learning projects, knowing how to schedule time for such endeavors, and knowing whether any progress has been made or anything has been accomplished, all critical areas in self-directed learning.

---

[8]Penland, Patrick R., *Individual Self-Planned Learning in America* (unpublished manuscript) Graduate School of Library and Information Sciences, University of Pittsburgh, 1977.

This entire concept of self-conducted and self-directed learning is important to leisure specialists not only because of large participation in terms of numbers of adults but because of its great flexibility and potential for use by all adults. It touches all kinds of adults and is very useful for the homebound, the undereducated and previously unsuccessful learner, the elderly, and the less affluent. Therefore, new service models, new materials, and new strategies and tools for adult use must be defined to meet the needs of adult learners in the field of free-time use.

CHANGING BEHAVIOR

(Learning)

Regardless of the methodology used to help adults learn, be it formal, informal, and/or self-directed, the focus should be on the individual adult and changing his/her behavior (learning). For significant learning to take place there has to be a real change in the behavior of an adult. Thus, behavior becomes the focal point of adult leisure specialists; questions like what is behavior and how does it change become primary concerns.

Combs and Snygg,[9] in their discussion of the perceptual theory of psychology, suggest that behavior is a function of how one perceives things. If an adult perceives something as important, he/she will behave accordingly. If the adult sees little value in something, another behavior will be displayed. How we see (perceive) the objects and events in our world will impact on our behavior and our response to the given objects and events. If, for example, adults see little value or need in useful free-time use, they will respond negatively to it. However, if adults see the need for good physical recreation activities, they will probably respond positively to them. If perception governs how we behave (as proposed by Combs and Snygg) and we wish to change the behavior of adults (cause learning), then we must look at what determines our perceptions.

---

[9]Combs, Arthur and Donald Snygg, *Individual Behavior: A Perceptual Approach to Behavior*, 2nd ed., New York, Harper & Row, 1959.

Five perceptual determinants have been identified: (1) Beliefs—what we believe to be true has much to do with how we behave; (2) Values—our belief about what is important; (3) Needs—(a) physiological—need for food, water, shelter, et cetera (actually our maintenance needs), (b) social—need for approval, status, acceptance, prestige (actually our enhancement needs); (4) Attitudes—an emotionalized belief usually about the worth or lack of worth of somebody or something; and (5) Self-experience—how a person sees himself/herself, how he/she feels about that, how he/she sees others, how he/she thinks others see him/her.

These five determinants actually form an individual's way of perceiving the world and, in turn, how one behaves. All individuals have their own perceptual or behavioral package based on their five determinants, and each individual's package is different, if ever so slightly, from another person's. Each individual's package has been formed from past experiences that the individual has had, be they good, bad, or indifferent. With individual packages present in all of us, each individual in order to learn must change that package as each individual sees fit. Thus an individual approach to learning is again suggested.

This perceptual theory has been applied to the teaching of adults in a previous work.[10] Since it appears to be a most viable way of viewing adult behavior and possibly of bringing about change in that behavior, it might behoove the adult leisure specialist to view some implications of this theory for adult learning. First, the five perceptual determinants are open to and can change. We adults can learn and can change. Perceptions are most readily changed through a reexamination by the individual of his/her own needs, values, attitudes, and the meaning of previous experiences. This, of course, makes learning a personal thing, and adults really change themselves. Adult learners learn in response to their needs and perceptions, not necessarily those of their instructors, and education should probably start with the problems of adults that are important and need-relevant to them.

Since needs, attitudes, and values are such important deter-

---

[10]Verduin, John R., Jr., Harry G. Miller, and Charles E. Greer, *Adults Teaching Adults: Principles and Strategies*, Austin, TX, Learning Concepts, 1977.

miners of perceptions, adult education must seek to help adults know what needs, values, and attitudes are important to them and to consider these fully in relation to each other. The education process should start where the adult is and permit him/her to determine his/her own direction and pace, and the instructor should relate pure knowledge only as it is needed and when it will impact on the adult's peculiar perceptions and beliefs. Also, to be effective instructors should understand the individual, and to do this, we should try to look at the individual and his/her world as the individual sees them. Finally, in any instructional setting the absence of threat must prevail because threat can restrict openness to perceptions and thus can reduce or eliminate positive change in behavior.

In effective recreational learning we really don't want a single, specific behavior, but an adequacy of perceptions and an openness to continuous experiences as a meaningful state of well-being in the individual is being developed. Strategies such as adult-centered instruction, group work, personal investigation, and problem solving can provide the kinds of lasting learning that adults want and need.

Perhaps a final point of consideration for helping adults gain new positive behaviors in effective recreational learning deals with the use of the three major domains, cognitive, affective and psychomotor. As suggested earlier in this chapter, the growth and learning in all three domains are important for a well-rounded adult. The cognitive (thinking processes), the affective (attitude and value processes), and the psychomotor (physical skill processes) should receive careful attention by the adult leisure specialist in program development. The early definition of goals in precise program building to insure that all of the needs of the adult are being met is important because sound goal statements are critical to the development of learning packages with which adults interact.[11] Without this attention learning experiences could fall far short of the target.

Adult learning, needs, interests, and developmental characteris-

[11]Verduin, John R., Jr., *Curriculum Building for Adult Learning*, Carbondale, IL, Southern Illinois University Press, 1980.

tics as well as the careful programming of learning experiences are very important for the adult leisure learning specialist to consider. Delivery systems and their professionals must observe these characteristics and interest needs and offer some sound learning experiences to adult clients in order to fulfill identified needs. Some organizations and agencies have made some handsome attempts at doing just this. Perhaps more should be done. However, what has been done by selected, major delivery systems can not be discounted and should be brought to the attention of those involved in delivering such experiences. A discussion of these contributions occurs in the following chapters.

SELECTED BIBLIOGRAPHY

Atchley, Robert C., The Social Forces in Later Life, Belmont, CA, Wadsworth Publishers, 1972.

Binstock, R. and E. Shanas (eds.), Handbook of Aging and the Social Sciences, New York, Van Nostrand-Reinhold, 1976.

Bischoff, Ledford J., Adult Psychology, 2nd ed., New York, Harper and Row, 1976.

Cheek, Neil H., Jr., and William R. Bruch, Jr., The Social Organization of Leisure in Human Society, New York, Harper and Row Publishers, 1976.

Combs, Arthur and Donald Snygg, Individual Behavior: A Perceptual Approach to Behavior, 2nd ed., New York, Harper and Row, 1959.

Corbin, H. Dan and William H. Tait, Education for Leisure, Englewood Cliffs, NJ, Prentice-Hall, Inc., 1973.

Cross, K. Patricia, Adults as Learners: Increasing Participation and Facilitating Learning, San Francisco, Jossey-Bass Publishers, 1981.

Cross, K. Patricia, John R. Valley and Associates, Planning Non-Traditional Programs, An Analysis of Issues for Post Secondary Education, San Francisco, Jossey-Bass Publishers, 1976.

Cumming, E. and W. E. Henry, Growing Old: The Process of Disengagement, New York, Basic, 1961.

Godbey, Geoffrey, Leisure in Your Life: An Exploration, Philadelphia, Saunders College Publishing, 1981.

Godbey, Geoffrey and Stanley Parker, Leisure Studies and Services: An Overview, Philadelphia, W. B. Saunders Company, 1976.

Goodale, Thomas L. and Peter A. Witt (eds.), Recreation and Leisure: Issues in an Era of Change, State College, PA, Venture Publishing, 1980.

Havighurst, Robert J., Developmental Tasks and Education, New York, Longmans-Green, 1952.

Heimstra, Roger, Lifelong Learning, Lincoln, Nebraska, Professional Educators Publication, Inc., 1976.

Iso-Ahola, Seppo E. (ed.), *Social Psychological Perspectives on Leisure and Recreation*, Springfield, IL, Charles C Thomas, Publisher, 1980.

Iso-Ahola, Seppo E., *The Social Psychology of Leisure and Recreation*, Dubuque, Iowa, Wm. C. Brown Company Publishers, 1980.

Kando, Thomas M., *Leisure and Popular Culture in Transition*, St. Louis, C. V. Mosby Company, 1975.

Kidd, J. R., *How Adults Learn*, New York, Association Press, 1973.

Knox, Alan B., *Adult Development and Learning*, San Francisco, Jossey-Bass Publishers, 1977.

Levinson, Daniel J., *The Seasons of a Man's Life*, New York, Alfred Knopf, 1978.

Lovell, R. Bernard, *Adult Learning*, New York, Halsted Press, John Wiley and Sons, 1980.

Lowenthal, Marjorie F. et al., *Four Stages of Life*, San Francisco, Jossey-Bass Publishers, 1975.

Maslow, Abraham A., *Motivation and Personality*, New York, Harper and Row Publishers, 1964.

Neugarten, Bernice L. (ed.), *Middle Age and Aging*, Chicago, University of Chicago Press, 1968.

Neulinger, John, *The Psychology of Leisure*, Springfield, IL, Charles C Thomas, Publisher, 1974.

Neulinger, John, *To Leisure: An Introduction*, Boston, Allyn and Bacon, Inc., 1981.

Parker, J. Stanley, *The Future of Work and Leisure*, New York, Praeger, 1974.

Peters, John M., *Building An Effective Adult Education Enterprise*, San Francisco, Jossey-Bass Publishers, 1980.

Peterson, Richard E. and Associates, *Lifelong Learning in America*, San Francisco, Jossey-Bass Publishers, 1979.

Rapoport, Rhona and Robert Rapoport, *Leisure and the Family Life Cycle*, Boston, Routledge and Kegan, 1975.

Robinson, John, *How Americans Use Time: A Social Psychological Analysis of Everyday Behavior*, New York, Praeger, 1977.

Sheehy, Gail, *Passages: Predictable Crises of Adult Life*, New York, Bantam, 1977.

Verduin, John R., Jr., *Curriculum Building for Adult Learning*, Carbondale, Illinois, Southern Illinois University Press, 1980.

Verduin, John R., Jr., Harry G. Miller, and Charles E. Greer, *Adults Teaching Adults: Principles and Strategies*, Austin, Texas, Learning Concepts, 1977.

Weiskopf, Donald C., *A Guide to Recreation and Leisure*, Boston, Allyn and Bacon, Inc., 1975.

Chapter IV

CURRENT RECREATION DELIVERY SYSTEMS

Introduction

AS WE SAW IN THE PREVIOUS chapter, raising the adult's awareness level of a recreational possibility is a major role for the adult leisure educator. A high-level awareness of recreational possibilities and benefits will encourage adults to act on these opportunities while a lack of awareness will help stifle the lifelong learning process. The purpose of this chapter is to review and discuss the major contributing organizations that currently offer recreational learning opportunities. Since the recreation field is characterized by a decentralized service delivery system, it is unlikely the adult leisure specialist will encounter one clearinghouse of information on all the services offered in a particular community or region. Instead each area's opportunities must be researched independently. This process can be a pleasant adventure for the adult educator for he or she might discover something of new interest. The following is a description of the major types of organizations.

INSTITUTIONS OF HIGHER LEARNING

There are approximately 1,155 junior colleges and 2,897 four-year colleges/universities in the United States.[1] Many of these institutions offer a variety of educational programs aimed at the leisure desires of the adult learner. One of the most traditional and widely offered programs is that of continuing education,

---

[1]U.S. Dept. of Commerce, Bureau of the Census. Statistical Abstract of the United States. Superintendent of Documents, Washington, D.C. 1979.

often called adult education or extension education. The programs normally consist of a collection of noncredit courses offered each academic semester.

There are three basic types of continuing education courses. The first type, recreational skill courses, is probably the most common. In this group one would find skills ranging from photography to cake decorating being taught by skilled nonacademic individuals. While some general leisure concepts will be discussed in these courses, the emphasis is on skills such as learning how to canoe, bowl, play tennis, paint, or play bridge. Such classes are a wonderful way to sample new recreational opportunities with the guidance of an experienced instructor.

The second type of courses could be termed life maintenance skills and are many times taken in order to save or earn money. Here we see courses such as home repair, automotive repair, home money management, and stock market investing. Other subjects of importance to life maintenance are dog obedience, child rearing, weight reduction, and self-defense. While many of these courses have a serious purpose, they can also be viewed as hobbies and most adults have fun while learning.

The third type of continuing education classes focuses on the liberal arts. The emphasis here is on intellectual knowledge for its own sake. Consequently, we find courses such as art appreciation, Bible study, American history, and psychology. Courses in nature study are popular along with foreign language courses. These instructors are normally from the academic world, and classroom procedures are somewhat formal. However, because these courses are taken for interest's sake rather than for a degree, students are usually less intimidated by the instructor, and the atmosphere is one of lively discussion and fun.

Continuing education is a large program throughout junior colleges and four-year institutions. With the population shift toward more adults, an increasing number of these courses will be offered despite the problems involved. Some innovative approaches are needed to adapt the formal classroom style of presentation to the adult's preference for self-directed, self-paced learning. The use of television and video tapes offer future potential. With the dramatic increase in home video players, the use of tapes will soon revolutionize the packaging and delivery of educational courses. One possibility is to use these home tapes in conjunction with a monthly class meeting in order to answer questions and to provide a human element. In addition to the television medium, creative scheduling of courses during mornings or concentrated weekends is a coming trend. Continual updating of course topics to be offered is a must. In short, the continuing education field has been slow to utilize standard, well-known marketing techniques to sell its product. Perhaps with a larger adult market and more fiscal accountability in the higher education system providing the incentives, continuing education programs will soon begin to adapt to the changing times.

While continuing education is the most extensive adult recreation education effort made by institutions of higher learning, a number of smaller innovative programs are emerging. One of these is the nontraditional student program. Nontraditional students are loosely defined as persons who are older than the normal college age and who have nontraditional motives for enrolling in courses. For example, most nontraditional students are not training for a profession and many do not even follow a specific sequence of courses within an academic major, but will dabble in a variety of classes, simply enjoying learning subjects of personal interest, a true recreational pursuit.

Programs for the nontraditional student focus primarily on recruitment. Once admitted into the institution, students enroll in regularly offered courses and, while some provisions for special advisement are made, in most regards these students are treated the same as other traditional students. The number of nontraditional students is small at present but certain to grow as a number of institutions promote the program in order to bolster sagging enrollments and tuition revenues. For the adult learner it is a nice opportunity to enter the academic environment at a later life stage without making a commitment to an academic major or a professional course sequence.

Another relatively new adult recreation learning program being promoted by higher education is the Elderhostel. This program, limited to individuals over fifty-five, was built around the concept of combining travel with an educational sojurn. Most Elderhostel programs occur during the summer, a popular travel time and allow a low enrollment time when colleges and universities welcome such activities. The course offerings range from liberal arts to outdoor adventure in which seniors put on backpacks, hike cross country, and even do some cliff rappelling. All the courses are especially designed for the senior clientele and focus on the fun of learning.

To date, the Elderhostel program has drawn an enthusiastic but small response from senior adults. Those who have participated generally praise the programs, finding the combination of travel, meeting new people, and learning a very pleasant and meaningful experience. Elderhostel is a national movement and as the number of senior adults continues to grow, this program should also grow.

Foreign travel combined with college courses is another program that offers adult recreational learning experiences. This program is built on a sixteenth and seventeenth century concept that encouraged young gentlemen to take an extended period of travel to broaden their perspectives and complete their education. Today's travel programs are, of course, quite different; but the core idea of broadening one's perspectives still remains.

While foreign travel is the main emphasis and attraction of the programs, a number of educational components such as lectures, tours, and selected cultural events are built into the itinerary. Some programs include extended stays at foreign universities and institutions where the participants are offered short courses on topics that coordinate with the travel route. Other programs are more like classical expeditions in which archaeological sites are sifted or plant specimens are collected.

All these foreign travel programs are normally designed and led by academic personnel. Most offer some type of college credit, and, in the past, these programs have been extremely popular with college students. However, with rising costs, foreign travel has become less popular and the clientele has shifted to adults, especially upper middle-class professionals who are able to afford such trips. For adults with financial means, educational travel programs still offer a wonderful opportunity to expand one's perspectives while having fun along the way.

In addition to the formal adult learning programs, institutions of higher learning host a constant flow of educational events and displays that are available to the adult learner. Seminars, films, and featured speakers on a wide range of topics are frequent on all college campuses, and admission is usually free or inexpensive. However, there are several problems that can restrict adults from taking advantage of the opportunities. Some programs are scheduled during daytime hours when adults are working. Parking on campus and locating the correct meeting room or lecture hall is not always easy. Information on the time and date of events often does not reach prospective adult learners. While all colleges advertise campus events through a variety of mediums, many times such information is not seen or heard beyond the academic community. Many colleges would benefit by establishing a central information office staffed by personnel who know all the campus programs and events. A telephone recording of daily campus events, much like the movie theater, would also be of tremendous assistance to anyone looking for programs. Colleges and universities have much to offer the adult community in the way of academic events; and many fine, important activities have been poorly attended simply because adults were unaware of the event. Much more needs to be done in this area to help bring the adult learner and academic community closer together.

It should also be mentioned that many colleges and universities operate museums and museum associations. In addition to various displays, museums, through their associations, will offer workshops, lectures, field trips, and a variety of educational experiences. One of the current movements in museums is to reach out to the public and encourage involvement in learning through programs. Here again is another opportunity for adult recreational learning experiences.

COMMUNITY PARK AND RECREATION DEPARTMENTS IN THE UNITED STATES

Today there are over 64,688 local units of government in the United States many of which contain community park and recreation departments.[2] Within their programs and services is a wide variety of opportunities for adult leisure learning. One of the largest programs that serves adults is that offered by municipal park and recreation departments. Modeled after the continuing education program offered by institutions of higher education, park and recreation departments offer a series of classes on a variety of topics. The emphasis here is primarily on hobbies and recreational skills such as dance, sports, or bridge. Health and exercise are also emphasized. Local experts are employed as instructors and classes are held in schools or other local facilities. In a well-run recreation department, a colorful brochure will appear three times a year—fall, spring, and summer—announcing classes to be offered. The brochure will also list special events, such as tours that are designed for adults.

Taken collectively, the educational classes offered by recreation departments provide adults with a fantastic opportunity to sample new recreational activities and broaden their skills. Fees are modest and class schedules are developed to meet adult time requirements. The only major criticism of this program is that classes tend to overemphasize physical activities at the expense of quieter activities such as antique collecting, art, or floral arranging. Traditional topics are offered year after year and recreational professionals need to be made aware of changing adult tastes. For example, home computers and electronic games are new areas that currently could be introduced to adults through classes. Adults and adult leisure educators need to assume part of the responsibility in keeping local recreational leaders informed through contacts and requests for new services.

Although it is partly true, it is unfortunate that the most popular image of park and recreation department services is that of promoting and managing a series of sports leagues. While adult league softball is the single largest organized team sport in America and involves millions of participants, organized team sports are but a small part of a whole spectrum of potential adult recreation activities when examined in terms of numbers participating. Swimming, with over 100 million reported participants in 1982, is

---

[2]U.S. Dept. of Commerce. op. cit.

the most popular activity, while softball ranks number eleven with 28 million participants.[3] The image that public recreation would like to project, based on professional philosophy, is participation in a variety of pursuits, physical or mental, active or passive, group or individual. There is a need to alert the leisure educator and the adult population to the great diversity in recreational activities, encouraging them to move beyond the sports stereotype and take advantage of public recreation services.

To help illustrate the above point, current recreational pursuits by adults can be classified into nine broad categories. A brief description of each category will help demonstrate the diversity.

ARTS AND CRAFTS: Along with painting and sculpturing, we find a wide variety of home crafts such as woodworking, decoupage, needlecraft, weaving, and paper craft in this category. There are literally hundreds of arts and crafts programs offered by recreation departments, museums, local clubs and other organizations. Many times art programs are coordinated and integrated with dance, music, and drama programs in a community performance. The National Foundation for the Arts and Humanities encourages adult participation in these programs and in the past has provided generous financial support.

DANCE: The word *dance* has a wide range of meaning depending on one's past association with the term. It can include ballet, square dancing, disco dancing, and round dancing as well as belly dancing and aerobic dancing. Dancing is offered by many different institutions and businesses. With a wide number of dance styles available, every adult who is interested should be able to participate in this activity.

DRAMA: Drama is usually thought of in terms of professional performances or children's skits. However, many communities sponsor amateur theaters in which adults find an outlet for their talents and interests. For those of us not talented in the art of acting, story telling opens a wide door to the world of drama. The vivid unfolding of a story is a dramatic activity that can be done anytime and anyplace, with one's children, relatives, or friends as

---

[3]A. C. Nielson Co., "Ranking of Popularity of Participation in Sports Measured." News release, Chicago, August, 1982.

the audience. Story telling, an almost lost art in the modern television world, is making a comeback and more adults should be aware of this delightful opportunity to do a little acting.

LITERARY, MENTAL, AND LINGUISTIC ACTIVITIES: Few recreational experiences make no demands upon mental perception or linguistic ability. In music, dance, social recreation, and hobbies, for example, there may be many opportunities for mental activity. However, there are recreational activities that cannot be categorized elsewhere that emphasize mental, linguistic, or literary efforts. Reading and book clubs, letter writing clubs, creative writing, crossword puzzles, and bridge clubs are some examples of this category of recreation. Meeting in small groups to discuss philosophy, religion, or current events was a once popular activity. Unfortunately, radio and television have overshadowed the art of debate and study groups are growing fewer and fewer in number.

MUSIC: Music is a form of expression that can be enjoyed by people of every age and every capability. For those with talented voices there are a variety of organizations such as barber shop quartets or choral groups that offer professional-type performances. Others find pleasure in small instrumental groups such as jazz bands, bluegrass or stringed ensembles. Some enjoy playing instruments by themselves, as evidenced by the popularity of adult piano classes. Rhythm bands, which are popular with senior citizens' groups, offer a chance to have fun performing. In addition, of course, everyone may sing in the shower or whistle walking down the street.

Listening to records, going to concerts, etc., opens the door to the whole world of music appreciation. Many adults derive great pleasure in becoming experts on a particular musical type through reading, collecting records, and attending concerts. The possibilities for adult learning in the music field are vast and should be encouraged.

OUTDOOR RECREATION: For some, the image of outdoor recreation is white water canoeing or mountain climbing, high adventure sports reserved for the young and daring. Often overlooked are activities such as bicycling, nature study, or fishing, which all occur in the outdoors. Camping, with over 61 million participants, is one of the most popular outdoor recreation activities. Camping can be combined with a travel vacation or it can be done just for the fun of meeting new people in an informal outdoor environment.

Being in the out-of-doors often brings relief from daily urban stress. Many individuals find deep satisfaction in quiet walks through the woods or in the study of nature. The benefits of nature appreciation, the sense of wonderment, peace, and contentment it brings, have often been described by poets and authors. Every adult should have the opportunity to sample the out-of-doors in order to discover the satisfaction or just plain fun derived from this setting.

SOCIAL RECREATION: This category of recreation is the most ill defined and difficult to describe. Basically it encompasses a wide variety of activities that adults do in order to have fun through fellowship. Parties, cocktail hours, picnics, and dinners are common social recreation events. A number of clubs exist that are primarily social in nature. These clubs sponsor dances, parties and other events that bring people together.

While virtually all adults participate in social recreation, it is wrong to assume there is little skill or knowledge in planning and conducting such activities. Creating the right moods to help people relax and interact with each other requires some creative social engineering. It could mean inviting compatible personalities to a small party or providing games and music to keep a large crowd active. Although some persons spend a lifetime refining the art of entertaining, most adults could benefit from learning how to entertain successfully.

SPORTS AND GAMES: This category of recreation carries with it the image of youthfulness and energy. Indeed, many of the popular team sports such as basketball or football are almost exclusively played by youth or very young adults due to their tremendous physical demands. However, there are a wide variety of sports that adults of all ages can play, and the concept of lifetime sports is important. Lifetime sports encourage active participation in a variety of sports that can be played over a long life span. Tennis, golf, jogging, or ice skating, for example, are activities that have no physical contact and offer the opportunity for each participant to develop his or her skills independently. More importantly, declines in physical abilities brought on by age are of little importance to lifetime sports. Each individual can continue to participate in his or her own rate and, by selection of appropriate playing partners, still experience the thrill of competition.

There are many values to sports and games. First and foremost participation can be fun. Second, competing with oneself or with another individual is a very satisfying feeling for many people. Third, sports offer a mode for release of daily stress and tension. Finally, sports help promote physical exercise. This last value is of utmost importance to adults who increasingly find themselves in jobs that require very little physical exercise. Taken collectively, sports and games help create a positive self-image.

The classical Greek idea that one needs to develop body, mind, and spirit reminds us that each adult has a responsibility to find some way to participate in physical activities. The key to participation is to discard the sports of youth that are no longer possible and to learn new lifetime sports. The concept of adapting sports to one's physical abilities seems quite simple, but many adults fail to get involved. In addition to teaching these adults sports skills, we must also widen their horizons and assist them in selecting sports activities that meet their needs and abilities. Therefore, adult leisure educators have much work to do in this area.

SERVICE: The last category of recreation activities is described as voluntary services or citizenship participation. These activities include membership on boards and commissions, service club functions, fund raising, youth leadership in groups such as the scouts, or visiting the ill. Volunteerism is a uniquely American tradition with over 22 million persons contributing time and resources each year in some type of nonpaid service. The benefits of being a volunteer are extensive and include social contact with fellow volunteers, a sense of satisfaction in serving others, and the opportunity to utilize one's skills. The latter benefit can be quite useful to women who volunteer while at home raising children and then later use their volunteer record to help secure professional employment. The opportunities for learning while serving others are great, and many adults have certainly received more than they have given by participating in this process.

Public recreation departments offer courses in many of the nine recreation categories described. More importantly, the potential exists to offer new and different courses that reflect changing needs of the adult learner. Classes for senior citizens, for example, are being developed as this group of adults grows. The challenge for adult leisure educators is to develop cooperative relationships with the recreation administrators so that both professions can help introduce adults to the diversity of skills and interests that are available in the world of recreation.

Getting people involved in recreation is a worthy goal, but the means by which one initiates involvement is the real challenge. For its part, the National Recreation and Parks Association initiated a "Life, Be In It" campaign. "The primary purpose of this campaign is to broaden people's concept of activity, and to get them to place recreation higher in the priorities of day to day living."[4] 'Norm' is the fictional character in the "Life, Be In It" messages on television. "Norm is shown sitting in front of the TV watching various sports programs. He tells us he is an 'all-around' sportsman as he balances his cool can on his 'beer bulge' . . . however, he complains that some of his friends have started to do other things—taking the dog for a walk, flying kits, going to the park with the family. He concludes, 'I dunno, we're a dying race!'"[5] The TV spots are designed to make it increasingly difficult for Norm to defend his sedentary life-style. Eventually he gets the message that it is important to be active.

The philosophy behind this campaign of promoting activity has been well expressed by Seppo E. Iso-Ahola.[6] He makes the basic assertion that the individual has pervasive needs for change, variety, and novelty. In seeking to fulfill these needs our society has adopted two general strategies. The first is participation in a wide range of recreational pursuits. The second is selection of a

---

[4]Editorial, " 'Norm' Could Just Sit There!" *Parks and Recreation*, 17(2):30, 1982.

[5]Ibid. p. 30.

[6]Iso-Ahola, Seppo. E.. "People Today: Withdrawing, Coping and Adapting," *Parks and Recreation*, 17(5):62–66, 1982.

narrow range of pursuits and adapting personal needs to what change and variety are inherent in these pursuits. The problem with the latter strategy is that a person who has learned to satisfy the need for a change through a narrow range of activities comes to view these one-sided forms of recreation as a necessity. "If so narrowly socialized with respect to leisure, the person is likely to overadapt to the environment, believing that these leisure activities are necessary for psychological well-being. Modification of environment and lifestyle... becomes such a painful experience when familiar patterns are upset."[7] Iso-Ahola goes on to state "it is hard to make a case for wholesome and characteristically human leisure in the name of the facts that the average citizen spends several hours in front of the tube every day and is predominantly a reactor rather than an actor in his or her leisure behavior."[8] Other social scientists agree concluding that active life-styles tend to produce more pleasure and reduce the loneliness, depression, and anxiety of isolation.[9] Another study found that "During the mainstream years from 20 to 50, those who are happiest and best adjusted are active participants in life. They are intellectually alert, socially assertive, engaged with environment and other people."[10]

The theme being presented by Iso-Ahola and others is that a life-style of predominantly active recreation contributes more to satisfaction than one of predominantly passive recreation. Being active in a wide range of recreational pursuits is the best way to satisfy one's needs for change and variety. "Life—Be In It" is more than a campaign, it's a mission with deep philosophical roots. However, as will be discussed in the next chapter some recreationists question the movement and its approach. In any event, adult educators should find the campaign and its philosophical

---

[7]Iso-Ahola, Seppo E., "People Today: Withdrawing, Coping, and Adapting." *Parks and Recreation,* 17(5):64, 1982.

[8]Ibid. p. 64.

[9]Gordon, C., C. M. Gaetz, and J. Scott. "Value Priorities and Leisure Activities Among Middle-Aged and Older Anglos." *Diseases of the Nervous System,* 34:13–26, 1973.

[10]Casady, M., "Character parts: If You are Active at 30, You'll Be Warm and Witty at 70." *Psychology Today,* 9:138, 1975.

base a valuable model as they design programs and classes to inspire adults to become active and reignite the learning process.

COMMUNITY EDUCATION

Community education, as a movement fostered by the C. S. Mott Foundation since 1927, has been an important promoter of adult education for many years. Community education means educational programs for all people of a community. "True community education attempts to fulfill the educational, recreational, social, intellectual, and health needs of people regardless of age, race, or limiting factors."[11] The general philosophy behind the community education movement is that all life is educational and that education requires active participation. The community education organizations use existing educational systems—local school districts, community schools, et cetera—to serve the whole community instead of just the traditional school-age population. They are charged with identifying the problems of the community and the resources available to solve these problems. The community education organizations then attempt to bring together local people to help solve these identified problems. As a movement, community education has been highly successful in a number of states, Michigan being the leading example.

The philosophy of community education as related to leisure and recreation centers upon the basic assumption that all life is education and that many recreational activities are educational. Community education encourages lifelong education to improve the quality of life. This type of philosophy parallels that of the classical view of leisure championed by Sebastian De Grazia. In his book he identifies the Greek concept of lifelong learning and improvement of one's quality of living. To the Greeks, leisure was synonymous with learning and was something one dedicated his whole life to pursuing.[12] It is interesting to note that Frank J.

---

[11]C. S. Mott Foundation, *Community Education Dissemination Program Manual*. Flint, MI, C. S. Mott Foundation (undated publication), p. 5.

[12]De Grazia, Sebastian. *Of Time, Work and Leisure*. Washington, DC, Twentieth Century Fund, 1962.

Manley, the physical education teacher who wanted to reduce the incidence of juvenile delinquency by increasing recreation programs in Flint, Michigan, was the person who inspired C. S. Mott to first become involved in community education.

Today community education has grown to be a significant movement. In 1977 there were over 5,683 community school programs across the nation. A total of 1,388 school districts reported having community education, and there were over 73 cooperating centers with a total of 119 university professionals involved. Total expenditures for community education in the 1976–77 year were estimated at 125 million dollars. In addition, eight states have passed funding legislation for community education. During the last ten years, the C. S. Mott Foundation has spent over 125 million dollars to establish new programs and to encourage established community education groups to expand their offerings and to adjust their programs to the continually changing needs of the communities that they serve.[13] While it is commendable that the Mott Foundation and the community education movement are making great strides in improving the educational programs in our local communities, it is unfortunate that the orientation of these programs has not included a stronger emphasis on leisure and associated recreational skills. Michigan, the state that has most fully endorsed the community education program, can provide a good example of the current program orientation. The Michigan programs have emphasized basic education in grades one through eight and a program to complete the general education development (G.E.D.) certificate. In 1977 Michigan awarded over 10,000 G.E.D. certificates and enrolled more than 80,000 students in over 1,600 classes, grades one through twelve.[14] This was the main emphasis on the community education program; the number of recreation-oriented classes and life-style programs pale by comparison.

---

[13]Storey, David S. and K. High Rolner. *The Historical Development of Community Education and the Mott Foundation.* Mount Pleasant. MI. Center for Community Education. Central Michigan University. 1979. p. 1.

[14]Columbus, Frederick. *The History and Development of Public School Adult and Community Education in Michigan* 1862–1977. Lansing, Mich. Department of Education. 1978. p. 82.

Although recreation programs are small within the community education movement, it would be useful to describe examples of some of the programs that do exist. Flint, Michigan, perhaps the leading city in community education programs, offers an arts and crafts program that has more than 400 class sessions annually and provides instruction in a variety of media for people of all ages, degrees of skill, and interest. A lecture/discussion program is offered that helps increase self-awareness and racial pride among minority individuals as well as improving understanding and cooperation among all groups. For the senior citizens, the Flint community schools provide a variety of programs and services to improve the quality of life for older people. More than 5,000 elderly men and women are served by this school system annually.[15]

Grand Rapids, another Michigan city with a firm commitment to community education has a leisure time enrichment program serving 16,000 people annually, in addition to the health programs for the physically and otherwise impaired and special education programs. A family involvement program, which focuses on adults and young people, serves over 500 people each year. For those sixty and older, there are several interesting programs including seminars on preparing for retirement; leisure time enrichment (with an enrollment of 2,500), a socialization program through the Golden Age Card Club (with over 7,000 enrolled), and a nursing and rest home program (with over 1,200 enrolled). These particular programs do focus on leisure and recreation as a part of the overall life-style enhancement program.[16]

Other cities throughout Michigan and the United States offer a variety of recreation enrichment programs through community education. The nature and variety of these programs depend in part on the availability of services through other recreation organizations, such as park districts, school, church or local commercial recreation enterprises. The goal of most community education organizations has been to complement and supplement those activities offered by the more traditional recreation providers.

[15]Ibid. pp. 101–105.

[16]Ibid., pp. 92–93.

In many cases, the community education organization will identify a program need and then, in turn, encourage one of the local
recreation organizations to provide the needed program.

In reviewing the literature, it is evident that the community
education movement could benefit adults by encouraging more
programs that deal with leisure and life-styling skills and in the
promotion of lifelong learning. They should emphasize the amount
of time spent in nonwork hours and the need for adults to learn
skills that will help them fully develop this aspect of their lives.
Not only is there a need to learn specific recreation activity skills,
but also there is a tremendous need to learn identification and
decision-making skills. By this we mean being able to identify
areas of personal recreation interest and then, in turn, using
decision-making skills to become involved in these interests by
allocating time and personal resources in a favorable manner.
Classes in the general area of life-styling and leisure life-styling
are very helpful in regard to decision-making skills.

Adults, as mentioned earlier, frequently participate in self-
directed learning. There is an opportunity for community educators to support this type of learning for leisure and recreation. For
example, an introductory series of classes could discuss various
leisure life-style techniques and recreational opportunities and
then refer the adults to resource centers such as libraries, recreation centers, or a variety of other local recreation resources that
the adults could, in turn, use in their self-directed learning efforts.
The community education classes could form partnerships with
these various community recreation resources inviting them to
the class for a lecture exposing the participants to their services
and, in turn, making the adults more aware of what is available to
them in their local community. An additional effort along the
awareness line would be the compilation and publication of a
local directory of recreation resources and opportunities. This
effort, in conjunction with the library, would be very useful in
helping adults select activities or topics they would then pursue
in their own manner.

In summary, the community education philosophy needs to
recognize leisure and the associated recreation skills as being of
equal importance with the vocational and basic educational skills

that they currently emphasized. Such a program in recreation and life-styling would complement these traditional programs that characterize most community education efforts. For most adults the years of intensive schooling in these basic skills are behind them and the learning challenges they face deal more with the free-time/leisure aspects of their lives than with the work aspects. This is not to suggest that continual upgrading of technological-vocational skills will be unimportant. Rather it is a call for a co-equal partnership between leisure and vocational learning. Hopefully, adult leisure educators will work towards moving the community education program in this direction to help it serve the total life-style needs of the people in our local communities.

RELIGIOUS ORGANIZATIONS

In the early part of the United States' history, churches were very antirecreation. The philosophy then characterized recreation as a diversion from the work of the church allowing people to play into the hands of the devil. Today, most religious organizations embrace recreation as a means to spread their various beliefs and also as a means of encouraging congregation-centered activities. An additional advantage is seen in recreation programming of people's time to encourage healthy recreation as opposed to undesirable pursuits. Consequently, today most religious organizations offer a wide variety of recreation programs. Some of the larger churches and synagogues have gyms, meeting halls, summer camps, and other recreation facilities. In major cities these large churches often hire professional recreation/religious directors who organize various programs and direct activities. Such a leader would also be active in managing a summer camp program.

With the flourishing of church recreation programs, there is now an opportunity for adults to learn many new recreational skills. By participating in these programs, adults have an opportunity to meet similar minded people and to form social groups centered around their recreation activities. It should not be overlooked that social groups are often important in carrying out a number of recreation activities requiring larger numbers of people. For example, bingo, church dinners, dances, picnics, etc., are more enjoyable when many persons participate. In this manner, the religious organization provides a basis for integration of its various members into the congregation. This is very desirable both from a recreation point of view, in which people support each other in their pursuit of various activities, and also from a religious organizational point of view, in which people of like beliefs are interacting and reinforcing each other's commitment to a religious doctrine.

Religious organizations also offer a number of opportunities for adult study groups. These groups often meet during the school calendar year and cover a variety of topics including religious history and tradition, health and life-styles, politics, and a wide variety of current social issues. Frequently such study groups are associated with retreats or trips in the United States or abroad, especially to the Holy Land. While all these trips and retreats will include some religious learning elements, the main theme is enjoyment and fellowship. In the process of having a good time, the adult has the opportunity to learn many new things, to see new countries, and to discuss various issues.

One can think of religious doctrine as a centuries-old method of life-styling. For example, the religious tradition of six days of work and one day of rest is a great champion of leisure. It provides us with one day during which we can and should relax. Though some religions prescribe very definite activities on this day of relaxation, it does provide a definite break from the work routine. On examination, it is seen that most religious organizations stress periods of quiet and meditation for contemplating questions of human existence and destiny. Indeed, to know one's God, one must relax and open the mind to a receptive state of contemplation. Relaxation is a commendable tenet to be championed by religious doctrine and the feelings and thought that one may have during this period can in themselves be considered self-directed adult learning. The pursuit of greater religious understanding has inspired many adults to learn more of their past history and tradition. In summary, religious organizations prescribe many modes of behavior for one's life, and this always requires constant learning and adaptation to the changes in modern society. One who is truly active in a religious practice is always learning.

INDUSTRIAL RECREATION PROGRAMS

Employers have been providing recreation programs for employees in the United States for over 100 years. Today it is estimated that over 50,000 companies offer various types of recreation programs, spending over three million dollars per year.[17] This number is small in proportion to the total number of companies, but it clearly indicates an opportunity for expansion of recreation programs and opportunities for adult learning experiences. Companies who do sponsor recreation programs find that the effort in organizing these programs ultimately benefits the company through increased productivity and increased profits. Most companies favor recreation programs for three basic reasons: (1) to improve employee-employer relationships, (2) to increase employee efficiency, and (3) to reduce the level of employee turnover as a recruitment and retention device. It has been found that happy employees make better employees, and the net result is a more productive, profitable company operation.

A majority of industrial companies sponsor recreation programs centered around activities such as sports, picnics, banquets, tours, and other activities. The opportunity exists for adults to learn and participate in various recreation activities as well as to learn of new areas through the various types of tours. In addition to these kinds of programs, some companies will offer adult education classes on a variety of subjects such as hobbies, crafts, speedreading, or whatever else is demanded by employees. These programs are very similar to the college or university continuing education programs but, in this case, catering to a very specific clientele—the company employees. A very interesting example of an education program sponsored by industry was the IBM program for retiring employees. IBM realized that most retiring employees live fifteen to eighteen years after retirement

---

[17]Kraus, Richard, *Recreation and Leisure in Modern Society*, Santa Monica CA, Goodyear Pub. Co., Inc., p. 275, 1978.

and therefore need new outlets and skills in order to continue leading active and stimulating lives. Therefore, IBM pays tuition for a number of classes beginning five years prior to retirement in which employees learn new hobbies or new business skills that may be used at retirement.[18]

Many companies are now sponsoring courses in health and life-styling. These companies, with large union contracts, are finding that health benefits have become a very expensive cost in the production process. If the company can promote better health among its employees, it will reduce its level of health benefit payments. Consequently, many companies are encouraging physical activities, good health habits, and good eating habits through courses and other forms of information.

Another large concern among many companies is a reduction of tension. Among high-level executives, tension is very common, and these companies are finding that a loss of one of these executives due to heart attack is a real loss of investment in time and training. Programs for the executive include classes on exercise, health information, and life-styling techniques, with specific classes on tension reduction being very popular. Since most executives are busy, new exercise facilities using isometrics and exercising machines have been developed that can fit into a large office-type room. These mini-exercise rooms can be placed in business office complexes making them convenient and relatively inexpensive.

Another aspect of adult learning in industrial facilities involves tours. Each year thousands of Americans visit the lands and buildings of companies while participating in industrial tours. The tours offer a wonderful opportunity for adults to learn about food processing, newspaper publishing, equipment manufacture, and a host of other production lines. These tours have become so popular that guide books are now published on available tours. The adult leisure educator should not overlook the tremendous amount of enjoyable learning that can be acquired in this manner, particularly during family vacations. What is needed is more awareness on the part of adults of the availability of industrial

---

[18]Ibid. p. 277.

tours and the opportunity to explore the world of work on a fun basis.

In summary, industrial companies offer a wide variety of adult education opportunities. In the future more industries will be encouraging recreation and adult learning programs, and adult education will undoubtedly be called upon to assist in their efforts. As more workers demand more satisfying work, adult learning and recreation will be an increasingly important factor in the total production process.

ARMED FORCES

The United States armed forces comprise the single largest recreation programming organization in the country. These programs for military personnel and their dependents range from sports and hobbies to travel. Within the base facilities and organizations, a number of classes are offered in hobbies, crafts, exercise, and sports. Travel and adventure clubs in which military personnel are encouraged to explore different cultures, are common particularly at foreign assignment bases. These tours, along with activity classes are a form of leisure education with the goal being to acquaint people with new and enjoyable activities.

Now that the armed forces are a voluntary service, we find that recreation has assumed an increasing importance in the role of recruiting and retaining personnel. Recreation has become one of the more important benefits that are available along with the use of the PX, health benefits, and job security. This importance of recreation has led the armed forces recreation personnel to reevaluate the function and role of their various programs. They have recognized the lack of leisure literacy among vast numbers of service personnel and their dependents. This lack of preparation in handling time blocks meaningfully has caused the recreation professional to question what else should be offered in addition to the "how to" programs and skill courses that are now available. Subsequently, the armed forces have made several changes in recreation operations. They now conduct periodic surveys to determine the changing recreation preferences among the various clients they serve. Additionally, they are developing a program of leisure counseling in which servicemen are advised on various opportunities for activities, trips, and so forth, and are encouraged to become involved in the pursuits most meaningful for them.[19]

Life in the armed forces is often filled with tension and uncertainty. Consequently, many of the personnel are in need of relaxation and tension reduction. For this reason, the armed forces are keenly interested in educating its servicemen on the importance of using recreation to relax and to regain strength and vigor. Like industry, there is an interest in reducing the incidence of illness and subsequent burden on health care facilities. Morale has always been an important factor; if the servicemen can be helped to relax and enjoy themselves, they will perform better while on duty.

Another important dimension of life in the armed forces is the early retirement that most servicemen take at about the age of forty. At this point, most officers and enlisted men will need a new job to supplement retirement income. Being able to make a midlife career change and to choose new work is an opportunity not many enjoy. It is very important at this juncture that the retiring servicemen realize the important relationship between work and leisure. The time and money domains associated with different types of jobs will, in turn, facilitate or retard participation in various types of recreation activities. Therefore, it is extremely important to examine their own recreation preferences as they search for a profession. Here is an opportunity for leisure educators within the armed forces to prepare retiring servicemen to make wise choices that will guarantee them not only a rewarding job, but also rewarding leisure, thus producing a rewarding life-style. Hopefully, in the future, the armed forces will begin providing classes to alert servicemen to the importance of leisure as they make their new career choices.

---

[19]Mundy, Jean and Linda Odum. *Leisure Education: Theory and Practice.* New York. John Wiley and Sons. 1979. pp. 174–175.

YMCA, YWCA

These organizations are often thought of as youth services. However, they do offer a significant number of adult recreation activities and adult leisure-learning programs. Most will offer a variety of classes on hobbies, health, exercises, games, and the like. Some operate community centers in which there is an opportunity to take a wider variety of classes in the arts, cultural affairs, and other programs found in a college or university adult continuing education program. Of course, participating in the recreation activities offered by these organizations will increase learning of recreation skills such as swimming, racquetball, and other sports. Many YM/YW's offer workshops on life-styling and personal health, and within these classes, there are topics on the importance of leisure and recreation.

These organizations also operate summer camps and retreats. The YMCA and YWCA are particularly noted for their various conference centers around the nation where religious organizations and national special interest organizations, such as the National Wildlife Federation, can hold conferences. Within the atmosphere of a retreat center, adults gather for both fun and education.

Most of the directors of these YMCA-type organizations are interested in increasing adult participation and are receptive to new ideas such as leisure learning and life-styling, that encourage adults to become more active and more concerned with their lives. Again leisure educators should not overlook the opportunity of working with this type of organization.

LIBRARIES AND MUSEUMS

Libraries, of course, are a wonderful place for self-directed adult leisure learning. Reading itself is a popular recreation activity. The world of books opens one's horizons to a vast array of new interests. There are books on leisure, books on time management, books on games, books on travel, and books on a wide variety of recreation interests and activities.

Many times one of the most important products of reading a

book on any topic is the interest that is peaked in a new subject. For example, it has been known that readers of mysteries become involved and interested in studying medieval history or taking a course on psychology. Accounts of history will cause people to plan whole vacations to visit historic sites or natural wonders. The world of books has this power to broaden our interest and wet our appetite to pursue so many things, and adult leisure educators must above all encourage people to find time to read. For those who, because of lack of time, money, or physical ability, cannot directly participate in recreation activities, books offer an alternate way to enjoy some of these outings from the comfort of their own home. As the popular bumpersticker quotes so accurately, "Jog Your Mind, Read a Book."

Not only does the library offer a vast array of reading material, but also it assists in researching information that might be useful for planning a trip, developing a hobby, and other leisure learning activities. Most libraries maintain a collection of vertical files with brochures and other kinds of loose-leaf information that can be very useful as one begins to pursue a particular venture. Many times libraries are a source of information on local organizations, clubs, cultural events, park facilities, and a host of other recreation opportunities available in the community. In some communities, the library may even have a staff person especially assigned to help people find "things to do."

Closely allied with libraries are the museums. Museums have traditionally had an educational thrust. The viewing of their displays and participating in their sponsored classes has as an objective the broadening of knowledge in a variety of subjects. Museum associations, such as the Museum and Art Gallery Association, encourage adults to develop new interests through their sponsored classes, field trips, and discussions. Many museumgoers have become interested in antique collecting, natural history, nature study, amateur archaeology, and a variety of new pursuits that center around museums and their activities.

Museums have always suffered from the stuffy syndrome. Many people regard them as places to visit once or twice in a lifetime to see artifacts that never change. On the contrary, museums are a very dynamic kind of organization. Their displays are ever changing and there is a new movement among all museums to reach out to people through educational programs. Adult leisure educators should encourage people to take advantage of museums and to rediscover their various programs offering a wealth of leisure education opportunities that many adults would find delightful.

SOCIAL WELFARE ORGANIZATIONS

A number of social welfare organizations include some components of leisure education in their services. Alcoholics Anonymous, for example, places heavy emphasis on the rehabilitation of recreation habits in its efforts to combat alcoholism. It has been found that drinking occurs most often during nonwork periods; therefore, this is the time when healthy, nonalcoholic habits need to be developed to help support the person in his or her need for abstention. We find that this organization has extensive programs on alternative forms of leisure, and that leisure education is essential to its particular cause.

Other rehabilitative services for the physically or mentally handicapped also focus on leisure learning. Many of these services deal with healthy people who have had a debilitating accident or disease and try to help the person make adjustments to a new life-style. One of the more common occurrences is the incidence of heart attack following which a person needs a complete change in recreation habits. He or she needs to relax and reduce incidents of tension and to find physical activities that will not cause overexertion. This sounds very simple, as a doctor's prescription might be, but these are very difficult changes to make after a lifetime of formed habits. A tremendous amount of leisure education is needed here to help these people discover new interests and to make new adjustments.

There are a host of other social-welfare types of organizations that deal with specific problems such as drug abuse, criminal behavior, and other areas. Each of these, while focusing on a specific problem, also spends time helping the clients examine and change their leisure lives. Criminal behavior, for example, occurs primarily during nonwork hours. There exists an opportunity to develop healthy recreational interests aimed at preventing a person from committing a crime simply because they were associating with a wrong crowd at a wrong place, a bar, for example.[20] Many of these social service agencies do not use the explicit term, leisure education, to describe their program when in fact this is what they are doing. There is a great need to help upgrade these leisure education efforts and adult leisure educators can help.

COMMERCIAL SERVICES

One must not overlook the multitude of commercial advertising services such as magazines, newspapers, television, and the like, that are heavily involved in leisure education. The goal of the commercial "leisure education" is to influence us to buy certain products. The theme of the messages, whether it be on television, radio, or in a magazine, is that in order to enjoy "leisure weekends" or "getaway trips" we must buy, buy, buy. Millions of dollars are spent by these commercial establishments to influence our recreation preferences. The attempt is to define what fun is in terms of the product being sold. The ultimate motive, of course, is profit. It is obvious, from the spending patterns in the United States, that the impact of these commercial messages on recreation patterns is tremendous. Few examples need to be cited, but one case in point is the new wave of electronic games and its impact on American youth. Adults are no less susceptible to this game mania; there is some doubt as to whether games are bought primarily for the children or as an excuse for the adults who secretly like to play.

Whether commercialism and its impact on recreation is good or bad is a subject too large for debate here. Advertising does educate the population and makes people aware of what is available to them. The role of the leisure educator is to make people aware of this advertising influence and aware of what is occurring in the media world today. The goal is to help people take advantage of commercial advertising and commercial services.

---

[20]Mobly, Tony. "The Bottle and the Tub." *Parks and Recreation.* 12(3):28–31, 1977.

Ideally, leisure education would help people become aware of their true personal interests and then have them use the media to assist in selecting activities that they like. This is a much healthier process, a much better guarantee of personal success in recreation, than letting the commercial world define needs and provide individuals with their products.

In many ways, commercial advertisement for recreation services can be thought of in terms of a giant recreation supermarket. Individuals should be able to enter that supermarket, select the products of their taste, and be able to take advantage of the specials without feeling the need to pick every item off the shelf. In short, adult leisure education needs to educate people on consumer selectivity. Here is a tremendous opportunity for classes on how to compare advertisements, how to take advantage of special opportunities, or how to recognize which heavily-promoted activities would not be in one's best interest. Such classes would certainly be of great benefit to a majority of the United States population.

The above discussion pointed out major contributing services to adult leisure education that presently exist. Although these delivery agencies have done a significant job, more can be done perhaps within a broader conceptualization of adult leisure education. The next chapter will focus on the leisure education movement and some new dimensions that might be brought to bear upon the existing situations.

SELECTED BIBLIOGRAPHY

Bammel, Gene and Lei Lane Burrus Bammel, *Leisure and Human Behavior*, Dubuque, Ia., Wm. C. Brown Co. Publishers 1982.

Brightbill, Charles K., *The Challenge of Leisure*, Englewood Cliffs, NJ, Prentice-Hall, Inc., 1960.

Brightbill, Charles K. and Tony Mobley, *Education for Leisure Centered Living*, 2nd ed., New York, John Wiley and Sons, 1977.

Butler, George D., *Introduction to Community Recreation*, 5th ed., New York, McGraw Hill Book Company, 1976.

Carlson, Reynold Edgar, Janet R. MacLean, Theodore R. Deppe, and James A. Peterson, *Recreation and Leisure: The Changing Scene*, Belmont, California, Wadsworth Publishing Co., Inc., 1979.

Chubb. Michael and Holly R. Chubb, *One Third of Our Time?*, New York. John Wiley and Sons, Inc., 1981.

Curtis, Joseph E., *Recreation Theory and Practice*, St. Louis, MO, C.V. Mosby Company, 1979.

Godbey, Geoffrey, *Leisure In Your Life*, Philadelphia, PA, Saunders College Publishing. 1981.

Godbey, Geoffrey and Stanley Parker, *Leisure Studies: An Overview*, Philadelphia. PA., W. B. Saunders Company, 1976.

Knapp, Richard F. and Charles Hartsoe, *Play for America: The National Recreation Association 1906–1965*, Arlington, VA., National Recreation and Park Association, 1979.

Sessoms, H. Douglas, Harold D. Meyer and Charles K. Brightbill, *Leisure Services: The Organized Recreation and Park System*, Englewood Cliffs, NJ, Prentice-Hall. Inc., 1975.

Weiskopf, Donald C., *A Guide to Recreation and Leisure*, Boston, Allyn and Bacon. Inc., 1975.

Weiskopf, Donald C., *Recreation and Leisure: Improving the Quality of Life*, Boston. Allyn and Bacon, Inc., 1982.

Chapter V

BROADENING THE DIMENSIONS OF LEISURE EDUCATION FOR ADULTS

THE LEISURE EDUCATION MOVEMENT

LEISURE EDUCATION, AS A TERM AND a concept, can trace its roots to the ancient Greek culture. In the United States it has been a part of both the recreation and education professions since the turn of the century. Indeed, the 1918 Conference on Education in the Secondary Schools listed the worthy use of leisure time as one of the seven primary goals for a secondary education. However, it is only recently that leisure education has become a movement of relative importance.

During the early years of the twentieth century, the newly-formed recreation movement embraced the idea of leisure education and sought to promote the goal of worthy use of leisure time. The common means to approach this goal was teaching recreation activities and promoting recreation programs. Many such programs and facilities promoted by community recreation organizations or departments sprang up in the period between 1900 and 1920.

It is important to note that the basic motivation behind many of these programs was social welfare. At the turn of the century, crowded cities and slum conditions caused social workers to worry about a host of urban-related problems such as integration of immigrants into the main stream of United States culture and juvenile delinquency. For these social workers, many of whom were our early recreation leaders, the concept of leisure education was seen as a means to promote better social welfare. While this is a commendable use of free time it is a distinctly different attitude from that which says leisure and recreation activities are of great importance themselves, regardless of their social impact.

While recreation departments and organizations were providing leadership in a vast array of programs and services, society still felt that the responsibility for leisure education lay primarily within the school system. Some of the school systems did respond to the challenge of leisure education, with summer recreation programs in small villages where recreation departments did not exist. However, very few of these school systems made an attempt to develop leisure education as a component of their curriculum. The usual approach was to offer classes in music, art, and an array of physical education skills. While there were a few school systems that did take an active role in promoting leisure education, most schools, even today, do very little along these lines.

Almost all the early efforts in recreation programs and leisure education were directed at youth. The world of adults was not included except perhaps in some occasional hobby classes. This situation is now changing as is our concept of leisure education. Instead of viewing leisure education as teaching recreation activity skills, we are now beginning to understand this concept as a continuous process of enhancing one's quality of life through examination of personal attitudes, decision-making skills, and the evaluation of recreation experiences. Jean Mundy and Linda Odum, who have written a complete book on leisure education, described the concept in the following manner: "It is viewed as a total developmental process through which individuals develop an understanding of self, leisure and relationship of leisure to their own lifestyle and the fabric of society."[1] The authors go on to explain leisure education by listing a number of points of what it is and what it is not. A sample of these points helps to fully illustrate the concept.

Leisure education is:

1. Deciding for one's self what place leisure has in one's own life,

---

[1]Mundy, Jean and Linda Odum. *Leisure Education: Theory and Practice*, New York, John Wiley and Sons. 1979, p. 2.

2. A process to enable individuals to identify and clarify their leisure values, attitudes and goals,
3. Increasing the individual's option for satisfying quality experiences in leisure,
4. A process whereby individuals determine their own leisure behavior and evaluate the long and short-range outcomes,
5. A lifelong continuous process encompassing pre-kindergarten to retirement years.

Leisure education is not:

1. A course or series of courses,
2. Only teaching skills and providing recreation programs,
3. The communication of predetermined standards concerning what is "good" or "bad", "worthy" or "unworthy" uses of leisure,
4. A focus on getting people to participate in more recreation programs,
5. Advocating a leisure lifestyle for everyone.[2]

The ultimate goal of leisure education is to enable the individual to enhance the quality of his or her life in the free-time domain. This goal moves leisure education away from the tradition of educating for a worthy use of leisure time through activity and skill development. Such programs were described in the previous chapter as recreation education. This was done in keeping with the distinction between the terms of leisure and education as defined by the authors of this text. However, not everyone in the recreation profession agrees with this view and there is still a large debate on the proper goal of leisure education and the role of the profession in promoting it.

Mundy and Odum propose two basic approaches to leisure education, "the extrinsic determination of leisure behavior and values, or the intrinsic determination of leisure behavior and values."[3] Following the tradition of early recreation leaders, advocates of the extrinsic approach believe there is a set of

---

[2]Ibid. pp. 2–4.

[3]Ibid. p. 4.

universal values and behaviors that are needed to realize the full benefits of leisure. For example, it is a popular concept among recreation leaders that a well-rounded person with a diversity of recreation interests is guaranteed more happiness and health than one who becomes involved in only one or two recreation pursuits. The "Life, Be In It" campaign, getting Norm up and out of his chair and into new activities, is an example of these values being promoted by recreationists. Supporters of the extrinsic approach believe leisure education's role is to develop a set of attitudes that are favorable towards leisure. They see these attitudes as central to the ideas of our society and champion them for the benefit of all.

The intrinsic approach, on the other hand, advocates the supremacy of individual determinism in a pluralistic society. Supporters of this tradition base their rationale on two basic beliefs: (1) the essence of leisure is freedom, therefore leisure education should facilitate individual determinism; and (2) leisure experiences are uniquely individual, therefore the needs of the individual should be the prime consideration.[4]

The method most recommended in supporting intrinsic leisure education is active facilitation. In the words of Mundy and Odum, "active facilitation advocates the intrinsic determination of one's own leisure behavior, attitude, values, and choices as a result of the systematic facilitation of decision-making skills and opportunities to think through and evaluate leisure choices."[5] Here, people are made aware of their own interests and how to pursue these through a series of decision-making and evaluation processes. In active facilitation, the professional promotes sharing and declaring of values rather than the transmission of a predetermined value set from educator to student. The supporters of the intrinsic approach believe the challenge of leisure education is acceptance of personal responsibility for one's leisure development. Again, in the words of Mundy and Odum,

---

[4]Ibid. p. 5.
[5]Ibid. p. 42.

"effective leisure living is solely dependent on one's ability to find dignity, satisfaction and integration of life in leisure."[6]

A MODEL FOR LEISURE EDUCATION

A time-worn principle of instructional design states that in order to initiate a comprehensive educational program, one must first identify the goals of that program in terms of terminal objectives and behaviors. These refer to the behavior a person should exhibit as a result of the instructional process. Mundy and Odum have formulated such terminal objectives in a model that outlines the scope and sequence of a leisure education program. Their complete model contains 107 objectives arranged under six categories and sequenced for the levels prekindergarten through adults of retirement age. Only the upper level is discussed here (see Figure 1).

Moving left to right across the figure, the first objective is self-awareness. Here the goal is to explore and identify individual interests. Leisure awareness, the next objective, focuses on the potential for participating in recreation with one's family, friends or by oneself. Once interests and potentials have been identified, the next step is to foster a series of assertive attitudes that encourage the individual to take action. Having reached the point of wanting to take action on personal interests, the individual requires a set of decision-making skills to select activities, the fourth objective. Social interaction, the fifth objective, examines personal relationships as participation in activities occurs. Leisure skills, the sixth and final objective, refers to recreation activity skills needed to participate in some activities.

In order to help educators implement the leisure education program, Mundy and Odum have gone on to develop a second model that gathers the objectives into clusters and then outlines methods of teaching. An example that follows will illustrate the approach taken here:

Objective. To be aware that leisure choices/decisions, like all choices and decisions, are related to outcomes.

---

[6]Ibid. p. 42.

Focus	Levels	Self-Awareness	Leisure Awareness	Attitudes	Decision Making	Social Interaction	Leisure Skills
	Young Adult	Reevaluates one's leisure as it relates to a changing life-style.	Recognizes the relationship between changing life-style, life situations, and leisure interests.	Analyzes life-style decisions related to personal goals for the use of leisure.	Takes advantage of the flexibility in personal leisure choices.	Evaluates social interaction patterns in relation to changing groups, roles, and responsibilities.	Utilizes present leisure skills and expands leisure experiences in relation to new groups and opportunities.
Leisure and changing life situations	Adult	Adapts leisure to compliment one's present life-style.	Balances leisure as a meaningful part of one's individual and family life.	Integrates personal leisure goals and attitudes into the family unit.	Makes meaningful leisure choices for self and family.	Enhances the quality of social interaction within the family unit.	Exposes family unit to a wide variety of leisure experiences.
		Recognizes one's responsibility and role in developing leisure concepts and attitudes within the family unit	Accepts responsibility for enriching community leisure resources.		Makes decisions regarding the enrichment of community leisure resources.		Develops leisure skills within the family unit and carries over leisure experiences from school.

Focus	Levels	Self-Awareness	Leisure Awareness	Attitudes	Decision Making	Social Interaction	Leisure Skills
Leisure and changing life situations	Later maturity	Analyzes the role of leisure in one's life as it relates to preparation for retirement.	Explores, expands, and further develops leisure in relation to changing life situations.	Recognizes the role of leisure in one's life upon retirement.	Applies the decision-making process in preparation for new leisure patterns and preparation for retirement	Reevaluates social interaction patterns in relation to changing groups, roles, and responsibilities.	Reintegrates leisure knowledge and skills into changing leisure life-styles.
	Retirement	Uses leisure to maintain a sense of involvement and satisfaction.		Adjusts life-styles to changing roles and increased leisure.	Chooses from a multitude of leisure choices, those most personally enhancing and enriching.	Maintains and expands social interaction with individuals and groups.	Uses skills from work and leisure for self-fulfilling leisure experiences.

Figure 1. The Scope and Sequence of Leisure Education. From Leisure Education: Theory and Practice. Jean Mundy and Linda Odum. Copyright © 1979 John Wiley & Sons. Reprinted by permission of John Wiley & Sons. Inc.

Focus. For every choice made, there is a resulting outcome. Making a choice and acting on the choice produces outcomes (results, consequences) that may range along a continuum of (1) positive to negative to neutral. (2) pleasant to unpleasant, desirable to undesirable (as well as other descriptors you may want to add). The purpose of this objective is to emphasize the fact that for any choice made, there are resulting outcomes. . . .

Learning Experiences. One interesting, poignant way to highlight the relationship between choices and outcomes is, without giving advance information, to involve the group or individual in various structured situations where choices are made that produce varied outcomes and then experiences are discussed. . . . [7]

Specific games and activities are then suggested to help integrate the material into classroom or informal settings. More details on leisure education exercises are available from two comprehensive sources; *Leisure, A Resource for Educators*, by R. Woodburn;[8] and *Kangaroo Kit: Leisure Education Curriculum*, Vols. I and II by Dorothy Zeyen, Linda Odum, and Roger Lancaster.[9] While these materials were developed for grades K–12, many of the ideas and exercises are readily adaptable to adults. Anyone wishing to pursue leisure education in a serious manner should review these two documents. As leisure education moves towards general implementation, with philosophy being translated into practical exercises, more of such material will be available.

THE LEISURE COUNSELING DIMENSION

The term *counseling* now carries many different meanings, but the concept originally started in the field of therapeutic recreation. As defined by O'Morrow, leisure counseling is "the technique whereby a professional person uses all information gathered

---

[7] Ibid. p. 66.

[8] Woodburn. R. *Leisure: A Resource for Educators*, Ministry of Recreation. Toronto, Ont. 1978.

[9] Zeyen. Dorothy. Linda Odum, and Roger Lancaster. *Kangaroo Kit: Leisure Education Curriculum*. Arlington. VA National Park and Recreation Association. Vol. I and II. 1977.

about a person to further explore interests and attitudes with respect to leisure, recreation, and avocational and social relationships, such as to enable him to identify, locate and use recreation resources within the community."[10]

Recreation therapists would assess the developmental needs of the physically or mentally handicapped and then would direct the client towards selected recreation activities. Leisure counseling, used in the therapeutic recreation mode, closely follows a pattern of the medical model; diagnosis, prescription, and applied therapy. A client–professional relationship is very much in evidence here: even though efforts are made to encourage client independence, the responsibility for decision-making skills lies heavily with the professional.

During the late 1960s and early 1970s the idea of adapting some of the concepts of therapeutic leisure counseling for the general population evolved. Vocational counseling, helping people select a job or career, was widely established both in the secondary school systems and the business sector. The question was asked: Why not develop a parallel service called avocational counseling, using many of the standard techniques but with a different theme—leisure and recreation? The idea blossomed and leisure counseling, as a popular recreation movement, was born. The clientele of leisure counseling was adults. The thought was to help those who lacked the information and skills to find meaningful activities during their free time.

Chester McDowell in his book *Leisure Counseling: Selected Lifestyle Processes*[11] suggests two orientations to leisure counseling, leisure resource guidance and leisure life-style counseling. The former is more commonly known as an information referral service. Here the client presumably knows his or her interests, but lacks information on recreation opportunities. The service in turn provides a wealth of information on places, times, and dates of various recre-

---

[10]O'Morrow. Gerald. A *Study of Recreation Service to Psychiatric Patients in Relation to Pre-Discharge Planning and After Care*, Ph.D. Thesis. Columbia University, 1968. p. 71.

[11]McDowell, Chester F., *Leisure Counseling: Selected Lifestyle Processes*, Eugene, Center of Leisure Studies, University of Oregon, 1976.

ation activities. Perhaps the most famous of the leisure information services, the Milwaukee model, was developed within the
Milwaukee school system.[12] This model is designed to serve both
youth and adults. Large computer banks containing a wide variety of activities available in the city of Milwaukee were assembled.
A leisure interest binder developed by Mirenda was also used to
help the individual identify the specific recreation activities of
events.[13] Upon specification of one's interest and available time
blocks, the computer would print out a list of activities.

The Milwaukee model was quite famous during the early stages
of its development.[14] The idea of a giant information bank,
computer accessible, was very intriguing. Today, after ten years,
the system still exists but has not been widely adopted by other
cities or organizations. Recreation professionals have realized
that information alone is not the key to helping people find new
activities. Value clarification, decision-making skills, and motivation are important components that must also be addressed at
the same time.

Leisure life-style counseling, the second of McDowell's leisure
counseling orientations, focuses on personal dissatisfaction with
the leisure/work life-style dimensions. There is a need here to
facilitate understanding and clarification of attitudes, values, self-
concepts and beliefs, as they relate to the development of an
individual's leisure/work life-style. Here an effort is made to com-
bine some basic tenets of life-styling, good health habits, and
recreation. Emphasis is put on both physical and mental health.
Recreation activities, eating habits, sleeping habits, work patterns,
and other personal endeavors are all molded together in an
attempt to design a holistic life-style that is pleasing to the
individual. Each component is dependent on the other; in order
to feel good, one must not only have satisfying recreation, but

[12]Overs, R. P., Taylor, S., and Adkins, C., *Advocational Counseling in Milwaukee* (Final Report),
No. 5D. Milwaukee, Wis., Curative Workshop of Milwaukee, May, 1974.

[13]Mirenda, J., *Mirenda Leisure Interest Finder*, Milwaukee Public Schools, Department of
Municipal Recreation and Adult Education, Milwaukee, Wisconsin, 1973.

[14]Wilson, G. T., J. J. Mirenda, and B. A. Rutkowski, Milwaukee leisure counseling model.
Leisureability, July (3rd Quarter), 2(3):11–17, 1975.

also good health. As in leisure education, leisure life-styling stresses personal responsibility for one's happiness. The goal of these programs is to heighten personal awareness of interest and promote decision-making skills. Retreats and group sessions are popular in leisure life-styling, where emphasis is on sharing of values and practicing of skills. The leisure counselor acts as a facilitator, restraining from dictating leisure values. As such, the counselor hopes to encourage individuals to develop and use the skills necessary to mold their own leisure values.

Leisure counseling, as a recreation movement, has been somewhat criticized by the profession. Many recreation leaders see it as a passing fad and maintain the tradition of providing facilities and programs. Other more progressive professionals see the value and necessity of promoting a holistic view of leisure and leisure life-styles. These progressive professionals are, however, skeptical of the methods and theories underlining the leisure life-styling movement.

H. Douglas Sessoms, in a recent article, asked some important questions about leisure counseling:

> Although most recreators ... consider it their professional responsibility to influence or direct recreation behavior, the question was, and still is, one of degree. To what extent should recreators advise, influence, or shape the behaviors and attitudes of those they serve in a direct, overt fashion? To influence and shape behavior when it is a by-product of our other professional responsibilities seems legitimate. But, when it becomes a central concern, then the issues of mandate, role, and legality become paramount.[15]

Kinney and Dowling, in a companion article, pose similar questions.[16] Both are concerned that many recreation leaders are intrigued by the words "leisure counseling" as a way to legitimize the profession and influence public esteem. Armed with a kit of tests, profiles, and group dynamic games, it is feared that many misguided recreationists motivated by a desire for power or importance will turn leisure counseling into a series of mind

---

[15]Sessoms, H. Douglas, "Leisure Counseling: A Frank Analysis of the Issues," *Parks and Recreation*, 16(11):64, 1981.

[16]Kinney, Jr., Walter and Dorothy Dowling, "Leisure Counseling or Leisure Quackery?" *Parks and Recreation*, 16(11):70–73, 1981.

games and quackish practices. Kinney and Dowling see the relationship between counselor and client as the more important part of the process. Viewing leisure as a state of mind, these authors see it as an "abstract and unique experience difficult to define and especially hard to counsel."[17]

SOME DIMENSIONS OF EDUCATING ADULTS

Many of us in the education profession have harbored some assumptions about learning that have caused us to employ certain strategies to use with adults in a learning situation. These assumptions have directed us, as we were perhaps directed, to some form of pedagogical treatment of subject matter and learning. Pedagogy, or the art and science of teaching children by definition, has been utilized quite extensively in adult education with not that much success and as such has been challenged as a viable direction for adult learning by Malcolm Knowles. Knowles in an early work has suggested that we should think more along the lines of andragogy, or the art and science of helping adults, as we work to assist them in changing their behaviors, and also mentions that there are four basic assumptions about adult learners that differ quite substantially from child learners. He states that

as a person matures, 1) his self-concept moves from one of being a dependent personality toward one of being a self-directing human being; 2) he accumulates a growing reservoir of experiences that becomes an increasing resource for learning; 3) this readiness to learn becomes oriented increasingly to the developmental tasks of his social roles; and 4) his time perspective changes from one of postponed application of knowledge to immediacy of application, and accordingly his orientation toward learning shifts from one of subject-centeredness to one of problem-centeredness.[18]

Much of the instructional practice occurring in adult education now has moved toward these basic assumptions about adult learning and in turn adult education.

These different assumptions about adult learning obviously

---

[17]Ibid. p. 71.

[18]Knowles, Malcolm S., *The Modern Practice of Adult Education: Andragogy Versus Pedagogy*, New York, Association Press, 1970, p. 39.

have substantial implications for the practice of professional personnel in the area of lifelong learning and leisure use.

Within the first dimension of the self-concept, the professional adult education leisure specialist should again, as Knowles offers, think about the learning climate, both physically and psychologically, to make it appropriate for self-directed adults, should utilize the adults' needs not the teacher's in the direction of the learning experience, and should plan cooperatively with adults in the direction of the learning encounter. Further, the teaching–learning experience should be considered a mutual effort of both the learners and teacher. The evaluation process should follow similar patterns with greater emphasis of self-evaluation by the adult learner. In other words, the treatment of adults in a learning situation is much different than the treatment of children because of the very nature of the self-directed adult.

The second major assumption about adult learners, their vast experiential background, must impact on the instructional process too. Adults, by living longer than children, have a greater volume of experience and many different kinds of experiences. These experiences may generally define what an adult is (or how the adult sees himself/herself) and can serve as a rich resource to continued learning. Adults can use these experiences to build new learning experiences if proper teaching takes place. It also should be kept in mind that adults will have more fixed ideas, habits, and general behavior patterns than children and may, therefore, be less open-minded. A more fixed behavior is apparent among adults.

The third assumption, readiness to learn, suggests that adults, like children, have developmental stages and just don't become adults at a given age and remain the same for the remainder of their lives. These growth or developmental phases are generally keyed to the social roles that adults play. Social roles of adults change as the adult moves from early adulthood to middle age and to later maturity, and the social roles of adults oftentimes dictate their learning needs and readiness to learn. A young married mother of a small child plays a much different role than a sixty-five-year-old widowed woman living alone in retirement. These different roles mean that different learning needs and states of readiness emerge; as an adult changes social roles, the need for different learning arises. This social role notion has great meaning for the adult leisure education specialist.

The final fundamental assumption associated with andragogy, that of the orientation to learning, is also most worthy of the leisure education specialist's attention. Whereas children have the perspective of postponed application of much of what they learn, adults are geared generally to immediate meaning and application of the topic under study. This, of course, leads to a problem-centered approach in the learning of adults. The immediacy of the learning is a direct response to some current need to improve some aspect of life, be it economic, leisure use, or whatever. Without some immediate application of the learning in the forefront, the adult will more than likely opt out of the activity.

The understanding and application of these four major premises of andragogical theory are imperative to the adult leisure education specialist. Without this conceptual framework, the specialist will more than likely function in a fog of confusion and misconception, especially in the area of leisure use.

Further, more evidence is emerging that indicates adults have quite definite learning styles; they have distinct preferences and dispositions regarding how they learn something. Smith suggests that certain tendencies and preferences of adult clients influence their learning styles and the way they would like to acquire new behaviors (learn).[19] In the process of acquiring new information, some adults would like teacher-directed instruction, others are self-oriented and directed. Some may prefer reading to acquire a new concept or idea, others may wish a logical, direct explanation of it, still others may wish to learn about it through audio-visuals of some sort, and finally others may wish to experiment or just "mess" with it in a hands-on fashion. Of course, some would prefer combinations of these approaches.

Also, in their preferences and dispositions to learning something, individual adults can oscillate on a continuum such as: being dependent—independent; talking—listening; doing—watching; being

---

[19]Smith, Robert M., *Learning How to Learn—Applied Theory for Adults*, Chicago, Follett Publishing Co., 1982.

practical—idealistic; accepting—questioning; individual—group-oriented; and 'self-expressed goals—instructor-expressed goals. All of these factors, of course, point again to the individual nature and individual differences of all adults. The understanding and application of individual learning styles and the dispositions, tendencies, and preferences by the adult leisure educator can make the task much easier and enhance greater learning on the part of the client. It will behoove leisure education specialists to grapple with and utilize this conceptual framework too.

Another definite behavioral package of understandings for the adult leisure education person to acquire in a formal or informal program would be the motivational orientations of adults for continued learning. There are direct implications from these for an effective lifelong learning and leisure use program.

In an early work generally referred to as Houle's Typology of Learning Orientations, three major motivational orientations of adult learners were identified; goal oriented, learning oriented, and activity oriented.[20] For the adult who is goal oriented, very clear reasons are identified, with the objectives achieved only through some educational activity. The adult who is activity oriented is generally involved for the social contact with people thus having no connection with the content of the educational activity and learning-oriented adults are basically seeking knowledge for its own sake. Although viewed as quite general by some standards, Houle's work provided a basis for further investigation in adult motivations for continuing learning by a number of researchers.

Morstain and Smart in a study of part-time students in degree-credit courses identified six factors:

1. **social relationship** a need for personal associations, participation in group activities, making new friends, etc., as well as being accepted by others and sharing interests with others.
2. **external expectations** seeking to fulfill the expectations of others as opposed to one's own intrinsic needs and desires.

---

[20]Houle. Cyril O.. *The Inquiring Mind.* Madison. Wisconsin. University of Wisconsin Press. 1961.

3. **social welfare** humanitarian concerns where individuals view their education as preparation for participation in community service.
4. **professional advancement** a concern for advancement within one's own profession; high motivation and strong competitive desires.
5. **escape/stimulation** participation in education as a way of getting relief from everyday boredom and responsibilities.
6. **cognitive interest** participation based on pursuit of knowledge for its own sake.[21]

Other studies have revealed quite similar results to that of Morstain and Smart. In an extensive review of the research on motivational orientations, Denton suggested that there were small differences in the factors that existed and offered the following synthesis on the major orientations of adults:

1. preparing for an occupational change or advancement,
2. seeking social relationships,
3. learning for learning's sake, rather than for practical reasons,
4. as a way of escaping boredom and/or seeking stimulation, and
5. using knowledge to help some sector of society.[22]

From this limited discussion on the motivational orientations of adults, several implications can be suggested not only for the utilization of the professional who will provide the leadership in this area, but for the entire concept itself. First of all, it appears quite certain that many people seek this kind of learning to enhance themselves, to do something to make themselves feel better about their own being and their world. They wish a better self and a better state of being for all.

Second, it should be quite obvious to the professional adult leisure person that adults are truly different in their motivations to learn in an informal or formal learning situation. Sitting in a classroom or other environment to learn something of a recrea-

[21]Morstain, Barry R. and John C. Smart. "Reasons for Participation in Adult Education Courses: A Multivariate Analysis of Group Differences." *Adult Education.* 24(2):85–88. 1974.

[22]Denton, D. Keith. A *Study of the Motivational Orientations of Full-Time Military Students in a Technical Degree Program* (unpublished doctoral dissertation). Southern Illinois University–Carbondale. 1982. p. 42.

tional nature could mean many different things to many different adults. Where one adult in a classroom might very well be interested in gaining some specific skill or bit of knowledge in a given area, another might be there for a simple social relationship or to meet others, a third may be present to seek some stimulation for a new adventure, and finally another might seek some application to help others or society in general. These multiple motivations will always be present in a leisure learning activity and could complicate the instructor's mission in the classroom; some people are in the class to learn very definite things and others could care less what substantive matter is being taught. The adult leisure education specialist must have this awareness and understanding in order to help adults to do something important for them.

Considerable adult learning takes place in a self-planned and self-directed manner, and much of the 70 to 80 percent of adult learning in this category falls within the domain of leisure use and recreation. This kind of learning activity not under the direction of a professional affects all adults—the very young and the senior citizen, the highly educated and poorly educated, the employed and unemployed—and is viewed as a very significant and popular way for people to gather new information and apply it, since as many as 90 percent of adults utilize this particular strategy of learning new things.

This popular methodology is used in many areas that can enhance the quality of life and the state of being of people. Again, it touches on hobbies, recreation, religion, personal development, the home and the family. This strategy can be conducted in homes, outdoors, libraries, and in discussion groups all of which are readily available to most adults. The motivations for self-directed learning clearly reflect the individual nature of each adult: individual pacing, individual structure and style, and flexibility in learning deserve closer attention by adult leisure specialists not only because of its popularity and individual learning accommodation, but because adults need help in this area.

In self-planned learning the adult must perform many if not all of the planning tasks that would normally be performed by an instructor in a formal situation such as the classroom. This puts the onus on the adult learner in terms of direction and help, even though other people can help in some fashion. This help can be of a sustained nature with outside people providing assistance three or more times.

Morris, in studying the learner's planning steps in detail, found that the first step was to clarify an issue or general problem.[23] An awareness of the need to learn or the decision to begin a project followed. Long-term, general objectives were established next, and then came the identification and procurement of various resources. Morris then suggested that beyond this point the steps involved varied greatly from one person to the next; no significant pattern followed.

In his investigation, Morris further found that the most common difficulties or problems in self-directed learning efforts were "1) in knowing how to start their projects (setting objectives); 2) in finding or making time to learn (setting objectives and scheduling) and 3) in knowing whether or not they were progressing or had accomplished what they had set out to do."[24] These are problems to which adult leisure specialists must address their attention for successful utilization of this methodology of adult learning.

To cope with some of these problems in self-directed learning, the adult leisure specialist could perhaps develop a series of checklists that would help the adult in—

1. identifying and clarifying priority areas for personal learning based on current interests and needs of the adults.
2. stating clear objectives that will provide direction for the adult learner.
3. determining and defining the appropriate methods, activities, and approaches to achieve the objectives in the time available to the adult learner.
4. defining a feedback and evaluation process that will help adult learners know when they have not only achieved the desired direction during the learning process (formative evaluation) but also when they have completed the process

---

[23]Morris. John F., *The Planning Behavior and Conceptual Complexity of Selected Clergymen in Self-Directed Learning Projects Related to their Continuing Professional Education* (unpublished Ph.D. dissertation), University of Toronto (OISE), 1977.

[24]Ibid. p. 195.

(summative evaluation). Built-in evaluation checkpoints during and after the completion of a learning project are critical for self-directed adult learners.

The above four points are most important and must be attached to, and depending on the nature of the learning project the adult education leisure specialist can assist the adult in, other things such as using the library, locating classes that may help, defining time to complete the project, and finding others who may have similar interests. The main factor here is to assist the adult whenever necessary in self-directed learning involving leisure pursuits.

The adult leisure specialist can make many other contributions, of course, within some sort of central, community-oriented, coordinating and administrative agency. This "leisure education community center" concept for all kinds of adult learning in recreation and leisure areas will be discussed in more detail in Chapter VII. However, some ideas that will assist self-directed learning will be advanced here.

Within a center concept staffed with professionals, paraprofessionals, and volunteers, such things as needs and resource assessments could be conducted for adult clients. With this information available, self-directed learners could be paired with volunteer or paid specialists for help, and a community resource directory could be developed to assist adult learners. Various materials such as videotapes, audiotapes, microfiche, books, pamphlets, and free materials could be stored there and could even be disseminated by some sort of mobile library and resource mechanism. Educational "Hot Lines" and "Dial-An-Answer" systems could be developed through the use of the telephone. Finally, this center concept could, through an effective public relations program, publicize all learning, resource, and consulting opportunities to learners through the media, and could provide leadership in the development of radio and television learning packages, both large and small, for additional use by community adult clients.

The adult education leisure specialist must again be aware of the tremendous potential available in the general domain of adult self-directed learning. This area can't be ignored in the development and enhancement of leisure learning for all adults.

This treatment of andragogy, individualized learning styles, motivational orientations and self-directed learning is cursory in nature, but does point out some very important dimensions of adult learning and growth. Tying in these dimensions and others could have a significant impact for offering a service in meaningful exploration into leisure learning opportunities on the part of all adults.

LEISURE EXPLORATION SERVICE*

Keeping in mind the goals of leisure education, the criticisms of leisure counseling and the special dimensions in educating adults, let us describe a service that has been organized to raise leisure awareness, while helping people become involved in a wider array of activities. This organization currently serves a population of college students, but the techniques can apply to adults of all ages. Many of the exercises could easily be adapted to a community leisure education center program suggested in the previous section. The Leisure Exploration Service (L.E.S.) assists young adults with their leisure needs by offering workshops that enable them to heighten their personal leisure awareness. This is accomplished by clarifying leisure values, organizing leisure time, or by simply assisting in finding the recreational opportunities that the local area offers. L.E.S. offers young adults an opportunity to develop an independent responsibility for choosing and making wise leisure decisions.

Since 1977 L.E.S. has served thousands of students, faculty, and staff through a threefold program. L.E.S. has compiled a leisure resource guide for the local community that serves as an information referral system. This guide serves as an easy reference to a filing system that includes information on a wide variety of recreation activities. Included in the file are the types of activities, directions, phone numbers, and other information for becoming involved in a particular activity.

---

*This section draws heavily on unpublished material developed by the Leisure Exploration Service. Office of Student Life. Southern Illinois University. Carbondale.

Leisure awareness workshops are the second part of the L.E.S. program. Both a two-hour miniworkshop and a six-hour (three two-hour sessions) workshop are offered. These workshops are designed to help young adults clarify leisure values, review how they manage their time, and explore leisure alternatives. The workshop format consists of a small group of young adults meeting with a group facilitator. Participants are encouraged to share their experiences and feelings with the group as leisure life patterns are explored.

The third part of the L.E.S. program deals with recreational skill development. The Leisure Exploration Service office is the place students go for information on the many programs offered to assist them in the development of their recreational skills. L.E.S. has information on sports club activities and instructional programs in every recreational area imaginable.

By examining the structure of the group workshops and the types of exercises used, the various issues brought into focus can be shown. Session one of the three-part workshop begins with an introductory ice breaker that helps participants become more familiar with each other and feel more comfortable. The first formal exercise is directed toward an assessment of leisure values. The participants are given a worksheet with the numbers one to twenty and are asked to list the twenty recreational activities they prefer.* They are asked to indicate which activities they like to do alone or with other people, the amount of money each activity costs and which activities would have not been on the list five years ago. They are also asked which activities need advance planning, which are initiated by friends, and so forth. Then, when this worksheet is completed, the participants break into pairs and share the information. This discussion becomes a very instructive exercise because many people discover that the things they like to do the most are relatively inexpensive, can be done with people or by themselves, and really do not need much advance planning.

Moving on to a further assessment of leisure values, a time

---

*This form along with others discussed can be found in the appendix.

management exercise is used. Here the participant is provided with a pie of life circle divided into twenty-four hours. Within each hour slice, they are asked to indicate times when they sleep, work, and complete other obligations. The remaining time periods are considered free time, and the focus of the group discussion is on when free-time hours occur and on how much time is available.

Now that the participants have explored some of their interests and some of their time domains, each person is given a worksheet with a series of open-ended questions. The group begins to explore and complete such questions as "If this next weekend were a three-day weekend, I would want to ..." and "I feel most bored when...." Sharing these questions with the group probes deeper into what values a person holds toward leisure and what kinds of activities the various members of the group prefer.

The final exercise in session one is called a guided fantasy. The group leader asks for total concentration from the participants. Members assume a relaxed position, begin a process of deep breathing, and through a series of guided statements become aware of their pulse, their body movements, and relaxation of tensions. Once a relaxed state is achieved and everyone is quiet with eyes closed, the leader begins to give a series of general instructions that help them move into a fantasy. The first instruction is to think of the place or setting in which the fantasy would occur. The next instruction is to describe the place in detail. Later, participants are asked to explore what it feels like to be in this place, if other people are there, and what sounds, sights, and smells are associated with the place. Eventually the group leader gives the instruction to begin to move away from the fantasy, and over several minutes the group is brought back to the present. This guided fantasy can be very useful, because within the freedom of one's mind a person will commonly roam through settings and activities that he or she most prefers. After the guided fantasy, a sharing of the ideas of where people went and what they experienced helps them focus more on their true interests. This discussion also reveals diversity of interests present in the group. Following the guided fantasy, the first session is completed.

Session two begins with a further clarification of values and then moves on to the issues of making decisions and carrying out new commitments. One of the first exercises is to allow participants to explore how others perceive them and their recreation activities. Each group member will draw a picture of himself or herself while participating in some form of recreation. Once the pictures are completed, the members pass them around to the group with each group member writing a word or phrase on the picture of what it suggests to them about the person who drew it. After these have circulated back to the originator of the picture, the participant reviews the comments and begins to see how others perceive him/her in that recreation activity.

Moving on to a values clarification exercise, a worksheet of rank-ordered questions that allows individuals to explore their recreation values and priorities is distributed. The members rank the answers to each question and break into pairs to discuss their answers and the ranking order. This is a standard value clarification technique that helps individuals discover their true hierarchy of values.

Once this exercise is completed, the workshop moves on to the topic of making changes. Again, the pie-of-life worksheet is passed out, but this time the goal is for each individual participant to design an ideal twenty-four-hour day. He or she will include what he/she will be doing, who he/she will be with, and where he/she will be, along with any other pertinent details. This perfect day will then be compared to the actual day sheet completed in session one, and a discussion of the elements and feelings that make up a balanced life-style will be initiated. This discussion begins to move the participant toward realizing the need to make some changes or decisions in his or her leisure life-style. At this juncture, a worksheet is distributed dealing with the steps of decision making. The goal is to familiarize the participants with the steps in a decision-making process while providing an opportunity to use the steps. On the sheet, a sequence of decision-making steps is outlined and discussed. The participant is asked what possible courses of action he or she might take in a hypothetical situation, and the group all contributes to the decision-making process. Then, each participant is asked to choose one of the alternative activities indicated on the "twenty things I love to do" worksheet, and make a commitment to the group that he/she will try to engage in that activity before the next session. At this point, session two is completed.

Session three begins with all group members sharing the activity that they engaged in during the previous week. As expected, some members will not have completed the activities they indicated they would. This immediately brings the group the problem of barriers. Here an exercise is distributed to help explore what these barriers might be. As a group, they will list perceived or real barriers that keep them from doing activities. The group will also collectively list steps that could be taken to reduce or overcome these barriers. Some of the common barriers include not enough time, not enough money, or not the right set of friends. Each of these can be addressed individually with the aid of the previous list of "twenty things I love to do" or the pie-of-life time block sheets.

Once the topic of barriers has been discussed, the group turns its attention to leisure assertiveness. Not only is it important to know one's leisure values and interests and the steps required for involvement, but one also needs to take action. Doing means asserting oneself, and this can be a very painful process, particularly in the initial stages of participation. First, an exercise called the leisure self-assertive scale is given to group members. This scale helps the participants discover how assertive they might be. The scale also helps initiate conversations on what is assertiveness, what are one's rights in recreation, and how it feels to not exercise one's wishes because of the lack of assertive behavior. Such lack of self-assertiveness is often a real barrier to participation, and this is explored in some detail. A list of leisure assertive rights published by Chester McDowell is provided to the group members and discussed.[25] Many times this assertive "bill of rights" is helpful in clarifying leisure values as they compare to work and interpersonal values.

The final activity in session three is a leisure auction. Each participant is provided with ten imaginary dollars to spend in the auction. A list of fifteen activities, such as a week's fishing trip to

---

[25]McDowell, Chester. "Leisure Assertive Rights." Portland, OR. A handbill published by Chester McDowell. 1978.

Canada, an all-expense-paid weekend to a large city, free rental of a color television for three months, etc., along with two bonus items are provided to the group. The bonus items are unknown to each participant. Each group member then must allocate the ten dollars toward those activities most preferred. Some people place all ten dollars on one activity hoping this will be the high bid since it is a most important activity, and they desire it beyond the others. Other individuals will allocate their money across a number of items hoping that they will be the high bidder at least on one or two. The process of bidding forces the participant to allocate their dollars based on their values. Personal leisure awareness, decision-making skills, and assertive behavior are all combined into the bidding process. With this exercise the workshop draws to a close.

The workshop techniques presented here are adaptations of many standard value clarification concepts described in the text by Simon, Howe, and Kershenbaum.[26] The assertive techniques are adaptations from a book by Lang and Jakubowski.[27] While these techniques were adapted for L.E.S. groups by professionals trained in psychology and counseling, the workshop group was normally lead by paraprofessional facilitators. The word *counseling* was never mentioned in any L.E.S. group; rather the emphasis was on group exploration of leisure values. It was found that the use of a paraprofessional who was also a young adult was most effective. Peers immediately are able to establish a great sense of rapport and empathy with the particular problems and concerns of the group. They emphasize group participation and group responsibility for sharing leisure values and exploring new ways to become involved in recreation activities. For the field of leisure this is an ideal approach.

To assist paraprofessional facilitators in their duties, the staff of L.E.S. offers weekly training programs that cover basic attending and listening skills, such as eye contact, attendant body

---

[26]Simon, Sidney B., Leland W. Howe, and Howard Kershenbaum. *Values Clarification*. New York, NY. A and W Publishing Inc., 1978.

[27]Lang, Arthur, and Patricia Jakubowski. *Responsible Assertive Behavior*. Champaign. IL. Research Press, 1976.

language, verbal following, paraphrasing, reflection, and initiation of responses. Skills in the areas of leadership style and basic communication are also emphasized. The facilitators-in-training experience a period of exploration and role playing to better prepare themselves for group leadership. It is most common during this training process for them to discover many new things about themselves that broaden their own concepts of leisure and associated recreation activities.

To date, the peer group leader has been a very successful component of the L.E.S., a concept that could be applied to any age group. Adult educators could easily initiate such exploration groups and through the use of some simple techniques begin to develop a following of leaders who would in turn initiate other groups and spread the concept of leisure exploration or leisure learning throughout a community.

The Leisure Exploration Service has served thousands of students, faculty and staff. At the end of each workshop there is an evaluation that has been uniformly positive. Comments are received on how group members have discovered new insights into their leisure values and new activities they may like to try. Each participant seems to leave the workshop with new perspectives and a sense of renewed commitment to try something different and to continue developing his/her leisure life-style.

SELECTED BIBLIOGRAPHY

Cross. K. Patricia. *Adults as Learners: Increasing Participation and Facilitating Learning.* San Francisco. Jossey Bass Publishers, 1981.

Knowles. Malcolm. *Self-Directed Learning.* New York, Association Press, 1975.

Knox, Alan B. (ed.). "Reaching Hard-to-Reach Adults." *New Directions for Continuing Education.* No. 6., San Francisco, Jossey Bass Publishers, 1980.

Smith, Robert M.. *Learning How to Learn: Applied Theory for Adults.* Chicago. Follett Publishing Co., 1982.

Klevins. Chester. *Materials and Methods in Continuing Education.* New York. Klevins Publications, Inc., 1976.

Knowles. Malcolm, *The Modern Practice of Adult Education—From Pedagogy to Andragogy.* rev. ed., Chicago, Association Press, Follett Publishing Co., 1980.

Knowles. Malcolm, *The Adult Learner: A Neglected Species,* 2nd ed., Houston, Gulf Publishing Co., 1978.

Knox, Alan, *Adult Development and Learning*, San Francisco, Jossey-Bass Publishers, 1978.

Epperson, Arlin F., Peter A. Witt, and Gerald Hitzhausen (eds.), *Leisure Counseling: An Aspect of Leisure Education*, Springfield, IL, Charles C Thomas, 1977.

Kaplan, Max, *Leisure, Lifestyle and Lifespan: Directions for Gerontology*, Philadelphia, Saunders, 1978.

Dunn, Diana (ed.), "Education for Leisure," *Journal of Physical Education and Recreation Leisure Today*, 47(3):31, 1976.

Wilson, G. T. (ed.), "Leisure Counseling," *Journal of Physical Education and Recreation, Leisure Today*, 48(4):31, 1977.

Chapter VI

PROBLEMS AND ISSUES IN LEISURE AND LIFELONG LEARNING

T HERE ARE A NUMBER OF ISSUES facing the adult leisure education person when viewing the possibilities of developing a
sound and effective program for all adults. Attitudinal, conceptual,
organizational, financial and personnel problems prevail that
when not addressed carefully, will definitely impact on leisure
learning experiences for adults. The following is a discussion of
these salient problems, which must be recognized, considered,
and brought to some degree of solution for effective adult learning.

UNIVERSAL COMMITMENT TO LEISURE AND LIFELONG LEARNING

When examining our societal commitment to leisure and lifelong learning, one has to conclude that there are a number of
problems. While Americans spend freely on leisure time pursuits
(the 234 billion dollars spent represents the largest single sector
of our gross national product), a number of facts points to a lack
of clear understanding of leisure and the support for its importance in our life-style. When defining leisure and recreation, most
individuals mention some element of fun, but generally fail to
assign any substantial meaning to these two terms. Many persons
are uncertain about the distinction between leisure and recreation and it seems that little thought has been given to the subject,
particularly in relation to the meaning and importance of leisure
in their lives.

There also appears to be a general attitude in our society that leisure and recreation constitute a natural human phenomenon, an instinctive ability to play, and consequently require little training or preparation. "We have in our society at present time, almost no concept of preparing people for a life of meaningful significant leisure. We talk a lot about it, but only a few have done much about it"[1] This attitude reflects the lack of commitment by our primary and secondary public schools toward leisure education. Although the worthy use of leisure time has been included as one of the seven cardinal principles of secondary education, public schools have done little to educate our children on this subject. At best the schools teach skills in physical education, arts, and music, but even these programs are the first to be eliminated in times of financial stress. Clearly the school systems are philosophically uncommitted to leisure education.

Normally, one would expect an economic sector as large as leisure to have a place in our national government bureaucracy. Unfortunately, there is no government agency devoted to the promotion of leisure and recreation: during the first few months, the Reagan administration summarily dismantled the Heritage Conservation and Recreation Service, an agency whose mission was to coordinate outdoor recreation. In terms of economic stature and national participation, leisure should certainly be represented at the cabinet level. The fact that it is largely ignored indicates a lack of political focus and support. It also indicates a lack of clarity of societal views towards the importance of leisure and recreation.

Perhaps the most devastating of societal views towards leisure education is the attitude that it is trivial. We have been culturally conditioned to assign great importance to our occupation. We train extensively to perform work and expect not only monetary rewards, but also personal satisfaction from that work. We do not know if we can expect leisure to also help provide us with a satisfying way of life. It seems that leisure and recreation are often relegated to the hours after work in hopes that with spending enough money and pursuing many diversions we will be able to enhance our life-styles.

---

[1]Staley, Edwin J., "The Struggle for Significance," *Leisure Today, Journal of Physical Education and Recreation*, 47(3):3, 1976.

While each of us certainly has the freedom to define leisure as he or she sees fit, this does not imply that all leisure values and ideals are of equal worth. With freedom comes opportunity and responsibility. One wonders if those who seek simple diversion during their free hours experience much more than a series of good times. In their striving for pleasure, are these people missing meaningful and rewarding experiences that would add a greater sense of satisfaction to their lives? "The rush to experience in our society which has brought about time deepening, and attendent diminished spirituality must be countered by the provision of leisure experiences which require commitment, sacrifice, and a progression of skills."[2] That many individuals in our society have only vague concepts of leisure partially explains their lack of commitment to lifelong leisure learning. However, this attitude needs to be challenged and changed.

Learning and self-discovery are perhaps the greatest of all leisure potentials. They add meaning to our lives and contribute to our personal satisfaction. Recent studies have shown that leisure is increasing in its contribution to personal satisfaction surpassing the contribution of work.[3] However, if leisure is to have meaning there is a need for a commitment to it and to lifelong learning. To counter this lack of commitment, three reasons might be advanced as to why lifelong learning in leisure is important.

It is well established that people change and grow through a series of life cycles. Each day brings new needs and challenges. Leisure needs also change throughout the life cycle, and there is a need as well to adopt new activities as we change. One of the greatest problems facing the American adult is the inability to make adjustments in recreation patterns during a life cycle. Adults often fall into recreation ruts, year after year pursuing the same activities. With this type of recreation pattern, it is no wonder we

---

[2]Godbey, Geoffrey. "Planning for Leisure in a Pluralistic Society," in *Recreation and Leisure: Issues in an Era of Change*, Thomas L. Goodale and Peter A. Witt (eds.), State College PA. Venture Press, 1980, p. 175.

[3]Iso-Ahola, Seppo E., *The Social Psychology of Leisure and Recreation*, Dubuque, Iowa. Wm. C. Brown, 1980.

observe diminished enthusiasm and vitality for living as we grow older. One cannot be content to learn recreation skills early in life and then follow the same patterns forever. Individuals should be prepared to continually learn and adapt activities to changing conditions. In short, leisure and recreation mandate lifelong learning.

If recreation ruts are boring and debilitating, an exciting and dynamic recreation pattern can have just the opposite effect. Leisure offers the potential for establishing an arena in life where success can be insured, but the secret of this success lies in defining one's leisure in a way that is personally meaningful. Many people fail to achieve a life of satisfaction because they are constantly comparing their standards and activities to those around them. In contrast, social psychologists have found that happiness is more a function of selecting personal standards and meeting these standards.[4] Thus there is a great need for educating adults on how to define leisure in a way that is meaningful for them, encouraging them to be content with who they are and how they recreate.

Finally, leisure offers an alternative for self-definition. Most people today define themselves—who they are and what they do—in terms of their occupation. However, as the adult population of the United States approaches retirement, jobs will no longer serve as models of self-definition. Even today with younger adults we see evidence that jobs are providing less contribution to the individual self-worth and self definition.[5] How can leisure and recreation help? If in a selection of recreation activities we begin to ask ourselves the question of what is worth doing, we begin the process of adding meaning to our lives. "Seeking self definition in recreation activities, however, should not merely be a matter of what one does but also an expression of what one is. Too often our society uses only proficiency as a medium for identifying and judging other people in both their leisure activity and work. . . . Self defining leisure activity is not at all synonymous with a level of achievements or the number of achievements.

---

[4]Ibid.

[5]Ibid.

How the individual does something may be far more important in terms of self definition than the amount of productivity or accomplishment.[6] A leisure philosophy that provides for self-defining recreation activities is not trivial. Such activities are important components of a full and satisfying life-style. They require personal reflection and a great deal of personal initiative in order to be realized. Self-defining activities require many personal skills. In short, they require a strong commitment to leisure and life-long learning. For this reason, the adult educator faces one of the greatest challenges in modern United States society, helping individuals establish meaningful and self-satisfying lives in the face of a constantly changing society. Failure to meet this challenge will probably have very undesirable consequences. In the words of Charles Brightbill and Tony Mobley, "The lack of planning and preparation for the wise use of leisure is more likely to crush individuality by allowing the individual to drift into patterns of conformity imposed by the mass media, the control and purpose of which may be directed towards other objectives."[7]

CONCEPTUALIZATION AND UNDERSTANDING OF PROCESS

In the first half of the twentieth century the recreation profession viewed the provision of various recreation activities as its primary mission. Leisure education during this time was thought of as simply teaching people a series of skills so that they might participate in a range of recreation activities. This philosophy of activity as the primary role of recreation has been augmented by what is now called a broker role. Here, the recreation profession provides its constituents information on the various activities available in the public and private sector. The role of leisure or recreation education under this philosophy is to provide people with an awareness of the information available on various activities. It can be seen that this particular role is now being assisted by

---

[6]Godbey, Goeffrey. *Leisure in Your Life: An Exploration.* New York. Saunders College Publishing, 1981. p. 291.

[7]Brightbill, Charles K., and Tony A. Mobley, *Educating For Leisure-Centered Living.* New York. John Wiley and Sons, 1977. p. 55.

local newspapers, radio stations and television stations that produce community activity releases.

While the roles of the recreation profession in providing activities and information are certainly important, the philosophers of the field believe a new role is evolving, that of enabling. Enabling as a role for the recreation profession means helping people select enthusiastically motivated activities that they wish to pursue. Here the concept of leisure education follows the Mundy Model (in Chapter V) of teaching people personal awareness and decision-making skills.

Intrinsic motivation is probably the most important ingredient in any formula for greater life-style satisfaction. The Greeks discovered that seeking and conquering personal challenges developed strong personal feelings of competency and self-determination. A key to the Greek philosophy was encouraging people to establish intrinsically desirable goals and constantly striving towards these goals. Intrinsically motivated goals have meaning for the individual, and striving towards these goals is especially satisfying because one can measure individual progress independent of other's opinions.

It is said that a person who is intrinsically motivated becomes a very independent and self-contained person. This is what is meant when some recreators say we must help people become independent of our activity programs. Independent and self-contained people are usually the most satisfied and happy people and this is the goal that we must all try to achieve in our leisure lives.[8]

The failure to establish intrinsic goals in our leisure opens the possibility of exploiting this leisure for other ends such as securing job promotions and achieving social status. The danger in responding to these extrinsically motivated leisure goals is that they may be unattainable because of a lack of competent personal skills or a lack of sufficient motivation. Fate or luck also plays a part in the attainment of extrinsic goals. Failure to meet goals or challenges often leads to a feeling of inadequacy and

---

[8]Iso-Ahola, Seppo, E. "Intrinsic Motivation, An Overlooked Basis For Evaluation." *Parks and Recreation.* 18(5):32–33, 1982.

lack of control over one's life. This in turn can lead to leisure behavior patterns characterized by mindless time-consuming activities such as excessive television viewing. When the extrinsic motivations of a job or social status are gone, particularly as a person ages, intrinsic motivations are what keeps an individual active. The unfortunate people who have developed few intrinsic leisure goals during their working life become restless survivors of the retirement age.

Adult educators face a tremendous challenge in encouraging establishment of intrinsically motivated leisure goals. We must begin the process of showing people how to develop intrinsically motivated life-styles. This is the key process in helping people maintain active, vital life-styles through their whole life span.

In addition to the concept of intrinsic motivation, a fresh prospective on the leisure–work relationship is needed. Since the industrial revolution, work has been characterized as important while leisure has been thought of as an after hours filler of our lives. This dichotomy of work and leisure is no longer viable, for in order to have a satisfying life-style, one must not only work well, but must also recreate well.[9] The key is to be successful in both arenas.

Unfortunately for most of us, our education focuses a majority of its attention on skills necessary to work well. The bookstores are filled with hundreds of paperbacks on how to achieve success and be happy at work. What is lacking is application of those same skills to leisure. For example, in the work world much is said about the importance of time management, which is also very important in the leisure world. "The notion of classifying and describing characteristics and requirements (e.g., cost, space, time) of leisure activities was a revelation to some. It had not occurred to others that planning skills used to maximize success in jobs were equally applicable to maximizing satisfaction from leisure."[10] Today many people face a problem of too many choices of

[9]Goodale, Thomas L., "If Leisure is to Matter," in *Recreation and Leisure*, Thomas L. Goodale and Peter A. Witt (eds.), State College, PA, Venture Press, 1980.

[10]Loughary, John W., "A Changing Perspective on Leisure vs. Career," *Leisure Today, Journal of Physical Education and Recreation*, 47(3):25, 1976.

recreation activities and not enough time to participate in all of them. Maximizing leisure satisfaction depends on selecting the best activity.

Application of decision-making skills commonly used in the work world to management of free time and leisure life-styling is an exciting possibility for adult educators. A thorough review of business curriculums, vocational counseling curriculums, and all areas of job training will reveal material applicable to leisure skills. Hopefully modification of concepts and techniques will not be extensive. The central problem is to make people aware that they should begin to apply these well-used skills of their work life to their leisure lives. This means the process of leisure education should focus heavily on examples of how goal selection, time management, and other similar skills can be applied to leisure. In summary, we need to educate people to seek challenge from their leisure; challenge that is intrisically motivated, challenge that offers a possibility for striving, and challenge that will provide satisfaction when the goals are met and the recreation activity is completed.

ORGANIZATION FOR DELIVERY OF SERVICES

If one were to review the literature or simply observe existing efforts, there is no question that many opportunities exist for adults in leisure and recreational learning; apparently there should be no lack of available experiences. Generally, those agencies or organizations that deliver learning services are many and basically can be grouped into four major categories: (1) public agencies, organizations, and institutions, (2) voluntary group-work agencies, (3) private groups, and (4) commercial recreational enterprises. Most of all these groups can provide actual recreational activities and opportunities to learn new things as well.

Public agencies, or those supported by local, state, and federal governmental bodies, include such places as educational institutions, community centers, parks, recreational buildings, and sports facilities. Voluntary and private groups, such as religious institutions, service, fraternal and social clubs, YMCAs/YWCAs/YMHAs/YWHAs, business, industry, hospitals, and the military, can provide learning experiences for adults, but usually on a restricted, membership-only basis. These agencies attempt to take care of their members as needs arise. Commercial enterprises, or those groups designed to make a profit from their services and business activity, provide some instructional opportunities for those adults who wish to participate in and pay for the kinds of opportunities offered.

With this apparent plethora of agencies and organizations to serve the leisure and recreational needs of adults, why then does this discussion occur in an "issue and problems" section of the book? The answer might be that all of the leisure needs of all adults, from very young to very senior, are not being met. Certain needs of certain people are undoubtly being met, but the needs of many others certainly are not. Why?

First of all, we are not sure what the needs of adults are in a given community setting. Needs vary from adult to adult and community to community, and without an adequate needs assessment we can not determine what adults truly want. We may never be able to satisfy all of the needs of adults since they have an insatiable appetite to learn so many things, but with selected assessment procedures we may come closer than we do now.

Second, there is no concerted effort to deliver the learning experiences required by adults. The leisure learning concept is dispersed throughout so many different agencies and organizations that it becomes uncoordinated and duplicative at best. It is not uncommon to have several agencies (i.e. community college, YMCA, Local Park District, Community Center) offer a class in aerobic dancing or macrame with partially filled classes and not offer too much more beyond that. This is expensive and limits the potential and efforts of the agencies to deliver needed services.

Next, how many of these agencies are prepared to offer leisure exploration and leisure counseling services? Most are ill-equipped to help the adult seek out a true leisure state of being. With these inadequate services the ultimate goal—a positive state of being—can hardly be achieved. We may do a great job of providing a softball league for young male adults, but are the other adults aware of and participating in what they need to live a more satisfying life?

Another factor that might be mentioned here is that of cost

and timing of the learning experiences delivered by the various agencies. These two factors plus location and transportation can become a barrier to adult learning. Are agencies, even with limited resources, taking these into consideration when designing the activities?

Finally, what current agencies (with the possible exception of the library) are prepared to help the self-directed learner in his/her quest for new and independent learning? Beginning tennis may be offered on Monday mornings and intermediate painting may be offered on Tuesday evenings, but when does a recreational agency provide guidance, direction, and materials for the adult who wishes to take off in a different direction to learn something not offered in any formal classroom setting? Since so much satisfying adult learning can take place in this dimension, which is so consistent with what adults want and should have, agencies can be missing a good opportunity by not providing this assistance such as was illustrated in the leisure exploration service (Chapter V). This important phase of adult learning does take understanding and trained personnel to effectively carry on the task.

The numerous existing agencies are working hard, again with limited resources, to provide for the leisure needs of adults. However, with better coordination, more precise activity, and a rethinking of what should be done for adults, better lifelong learning for adults could occur, which can lead to a more satisfying state of being for all.

LIMITED RESOURCES

Another major concern that plagues the concept of lifelong learning and effective leisure use is that of limited resources. Resources of all sorts, fiscal, spatial, and nonrenewable, are limited and this complicates effective developmental activities. Much of the support for both leisure and recreational activities and adult and continuing education comes from the government, such as local, state, and federal agencies. The basic ingredient of the support, money, is not forthcoming, which reflects a definite attitude and a lack of priority in these important areas. The taxpayers' revolt might be suggested as evidence in this case.

Many recreational facilities supported by governmental agencies are inadequate, abused, overcrowded, understaffed, and antiquated. Space, particularly in urban areas, is limited and needs revamping. Abuses to existing parks, playgrounds, and even such entities as the Great Lakes complicate matters for professionals. Energy to travel to distant recreational areas away from the cities has become expensive and has precluded some activities. The corollary to this is that many facilities in urban areas where about two-thirds of our population reside are inadequate to meet large numbers of people. Many national parks of status have become overcrowded and understaffed. And, older recreational facilities developed in the 1930s that met earlier needs of people are not compatible with a contemporary, ever-changing society. To cope with many of these problems the governing agencies have to compete for funds with other agencies and generally don't fare well, again because of expressed priorities.

In the general field of adult and continuing education, the areas of leisure, self-enhancement, and self-enrichment do not fare well in terms of resource allocation either. This too can be attributed to a lack of priority in the area. As mentioned earlier, the massive area of vocational-technical-occupational training and improvement leads the way in terms of total numbers of participants, course offerings and amounts of money expended. Achieving degress, certificates, and licenses, which also has an economic motivation, is another large area of involvement and expenditure in the lifelong learning process. Leisure and self-enrichment learning experiences are, as might be expected, the least popular ones in the field. It should be kept in mind that these choices for learning experiences are made, of course, by adults, as adults are not truly forced into classes. However, priorities are reflected by the various agencies and organizations that offer learning experiences.

In some cases public community colleges may not receive any state monetary reimbursement for these "fun and games" classes and offer them only as a "community service." Whereas a community college is reimbursed by a state department for vocational-technical courses or adult basic education courses or general education courses, it may not receive any funding for a course in photography or macrame or aerobic dancing. In religious institutions considerable time, money, and energy are expended for religious learning for children and youth; but, in comparison, programs to enrich the adult are barely existent. Formal learning programs in the military, correctional institutions, and business and industry reflect a similar lack of priority and funding in the areas of leisure and self-enhancement. With limited resources reflected by a case of low priority and value, the professional adult leisure education specialist will have a most difficult time developing the area to a position of truly helping adults.

PROFESSIONAL PERSONNEL

Another issue in the development of an effective lifelong learning and leisure use program for adults is the preparation of professional personnel to provide the required leadership for the process. A number of expert recreationists and adult educationists are presently on the contemporary scene who are quite able to carry on their respective functions. In the area of recreation, people have been trained to carry on the functions of an effective leisure-use program for all ages, early childhood to senior citizens. Neulinger has identified four major categories of professional involvement needed to develop effective recreational programs and suggests that this involvement ranges from information delivery to motivational activity.[11] The four types, leisure resources consulting, leisure education, leisure counseling, and leisure therapy, require college-trained people at varying levels because of different duties and responsibilities in the leisure domain. These people, it is assumed, would have a thorough grounding in the theory and practice of leisure. However, to carry out an effective learning effort and to make a significant behavioral change in adults, some further training may be required on the parts of these potential professionals; a newer type of individual may need to be developed.

---

[11]Neulinger, John. *To Leisure: An Introduction.* Boston. Allyn & Bacon, Inc., 1981.

The person who works with adults in learning situations must understand, among other things, adult developmental stages, values, motivations, goals, and learning styles. Particularly, this person must look carefully at teaching–learning strategies as they pertain to adult characteristics and their impact on learning. Since we work in a purely voluntary, noncompulsory educational environment, we must become aware of a number of factors that will have an impact on our educational endeavors.

To accomplish this task of preparing professional people for different positions, an emphasis for acquiring new behaviors can be placed at both the preservice and in-service levels. For the preservice, courses and experiences at the bachelor's as well as the graduate level must be developed to learn about the philosophy of adult leisure education, the nature, learning, developmental stages, and motivations of adults, the strategies for assisting adults in learning, the organization and administration of adult leisure learning, and the processes involved in the total concept. Indepth study of major topics along with clinical and field experiences could help develop the kind of professional required to carry out the mission. Program development work by both leisure and recreation specialists and adult education specialists will be required to foster these learning experiences for prospective professionals.

For the in-service levels, needs assessments could be conducted to ascertain the knowledge and skill levels of practicing professionals, and then a move to an effective staff development program should be instituted. Staff development for professionals "is defined as both the process of planning and implementing programs for members with an emphasis of behavior, attitudes, and conditions for the improvement of job performance and capability in an organization."[12] A total concept of staff development will thus lead to the overall improvement and effectiveness of the professional personnel and the agency or organization in which they work. Appropriate workshops, seminars, training sessions, and courses could be developed, implemented and

---

[12]Miller, Harry G. and John R. Verduin, Jr., *The Adult Educator: A Handbook for Staff Development*. Houston, Gulf Publishing Co., 1979, p. 4.

evaluated to meet the expressed needs of the professionals and governing agencies.

Although many of the problems inherent in the development and maintenance of an effective, lifelong leisure-learning program for adults may seem insurmountable, a number of ideas can be advanced that could move the process toward fruition. Some ideas include value reorientation and education, and some involve different organizational patterns of existing services or the development of new services for adult learning in leisure education. The following, concluding chapter addresses its attention to this matter.

SELECTED BIBLIOGRAPHY

American Alliance for Health, Physical Education and Recreation, *Leisure Today: Selective Readings*, AAHPER, Washington, D.C., 1980.

Darkenwald, Gordon G. and Sharan Merriam, *Adult Education: Foundations of Practice*, New York, Harper and Row Publishers, 1982.

Elias, John L. and Sharan Merriam, *Philosophical Foundations of Adult Education*, Huntington, NY, Robert E. Krieger Publishing Co., 1980.

Houle, Cyril O., *Continuing Learning in the Professions*, San Francisco, Jossey-Bass Publishers, 1980.

Iso-Ahola, Seppo E. (ed.), *Social Psychological Perspectives on Leisure and Recreation*, Springfield, IL, Charles C Thomas, 1980.

Kaplan, Max, and Phillip Bosserman (eds.), *Technology, Human Values and Leisure*, Nashville, Abingdon Press, 1972.

Miller, Harry G. and John R. Verduin, Jr., *The Adult Educator: A Handbook for Staff Development*, Houston, Gulf Publishing Co., 1979.

Neulinger, John, *To Leisure: An Introduction*, Boston, Allyn and Bacon, Inc., 1981.

Rauch, David B., *Priorities in Adult Education*, New York, Macmillan Publishing Company, Inc., 1972.

Roberts, Kenneth, *Contemporary Society and the Growth of Leisure*, New York, Longman Inc., 1978.

Weiskopf, Donald C., *Recreation and Leisure: Improving the Quality of Life*, Boston, Allyn and Bacon, Inc., 1982.

Chapter VII

DIRECTIONS FOR LEISURE AND LIFELONG LEARNING

DEVELOPMENT OF A LEISURE ETHIC AND VALUE SYSTEM

EDUCATION CAN HAVE ONLY ONE PRIMARY aim—Education for Living. This quote appeared in the book by Brightbill and Mobley *Education for Leisure Center Living.*[1] Since leisure comprises a significant portion of our lives, institutions of public education and others need to build a leisure ethic and value system that will guide us in the use of our free time. When considering the problem of educating for leisure the question arises of how to help both young students and adult learners transfer leisure values presented through classroom material into real life experiences. If it were a matter of teaching a hobby or a skill or showing information concerning current available activities, the task would be very easy. However, in order to make leisure values applicable, we have to build deeper understanding of how these activities relate to the strengthening of personality and to the quality of living. What we need in education is a rearrangement of our leisure and recreation values.

Rearrangement of values is a process not totally understood in our society. However social scientists tell us that beliefs and attitudes are very important as we attempt changing these leisure values.[2] Beliefs as defined by the social psychologist are the

---

[1]Brightbill. Charles K. and Tony Mobley, *Education for Leisure Centered Living,* 2nd ed.. New York. John Wiley and Sons. 1977. p. 64.

[2]Iso-Ahola. Seppo E.. *The Social Psychology of Leisure and Recreation*. Dubuque. Iowa. William C. Brown. 1980.

amount of information a person has about an object or subject. Attitudes, on the other hand, are a learned predisposition to respond in a favorable or unfavorable manner in respect to an activity or situation. Beliefs influence and form the basis for our attitudes. In the case of leisure, beliefs about the personal values of leisure and how it will enrich our lives will lead to a favorable attitude toward leisure. This favorable attitude will in turn predispose us to use our resources and free time to engage in a number of activities. It seems, therefore, the key to building a leisure ethic begins with an examination of our beliefs towards leisure. A question concerns the role public schools play in helping formulate leisure beliefs. After examining the public schools' efforts toward building leisure values, some recreation leaders feel that more curriculum and emphasis should be devoted to this topic. "Just as learning of math is fundamental to engineering, so is learning about art, sport, and music fundamental to individual fulfillment. Schools should require more production in the so-called nonproductive activities; increased amounts of discretionary time require it. Whether individuals will ever use these skills is no more certain than our current application of algebraic formulae to everyday living activities, yet we spend hundreds of hours each year teaching students how to do mathematics on the assumption that they need it."[3] In addition to teaching activity skills, the public schools can help build leisure values by making the educational process reflect a leisure ethic. Schools, for instance, should not look like factories. Classrooms can be more attractive and individualized with plants, fish displays, and exhibits of the children's art. There should be time periods not rigidly scheduled during which contemplation or daydreaming could take place. There should be opportunities for children to volunteer their help. Several years ago it was reported in the news that one school system instituted a half hour of reading in which all children, teachers, administrators, and secretaries would spend the designated time reading whatever material they wished. The idea soon gained overwhelming popularity, and it was discovered that the

---

[3]Sessoms, Douglas H., "The Impossible Dream?" *Leisure Today Journal of Physical Education and Recreation*, 47(3):38, 1976.

students were reading more and becoming much better informed. By introducing reading as a fun activity, students not only discovered its leisure value, but also learned something.

There are other suggestions of how to integrate leisure beliefs into the standard curriculum. When careers are discussed, mention should be made of the recreation possibilities that accompany these careers. For example, a fireman may earn less than a physician, but certainly has abundant free time. The recreation possibilities of both these jobs are quite different. In the area of arts and crafts children should be encouraged to participate and create artistic expressions that have meaning for themselves. Afterwards it is most important to discuss the pleasure they derive from these activities. Works of art created by adults should also be brought into the classroom to demonstrate how these activities can be meaningful to people of all ages and how they can be enjoyed throughout their lives.

Music appreciation has always been taught in the schools, but the benefits of music appreciation need more emphasis. Music can be used to provide rest and relaxation. Music can be used to provide stimulation and activity. Children should be alerted to how parents use music in their home and how they themselves can use it depending on their moods and their needs. The value of public television and that it is fun to learn through this medium could be pointed out in the classroom.

While many of us would like to believe that public schools are instrumental in formulating lifelong beliefs, it must be pointed out that there are a number of limitations that make it difficult for schools to have any lasting impact on a student's leisure beliefs. First, many forms of recreation cannot be fully appreciated until people have obtained physical, emotional, and social maturity. Second, new technological and social developments are constantly modifying the range of available recreation activities, and it is difficult to anticipate future leisure needs. Third, schools historically emphasize competitive and group activities. However, we find that many adults prefer noncompetitive recreation activities done individually or in the company of small groups. Finally we must realize that as children mature their leisure beliefs will change as new information and experiences are gathered.

Each of the four points serves to limit to some degree the impact that schools will have on our lifetime leisure beliefs. While it is evident that leisure beliefs begin forming during the early childhood years and positive beliefs held at this stage will help develop favorable attitudes towards leisure in adulthood, we must realize that the process of education cannot stop with the public schools. In a sense, our early years in public schools and at home should prepare us to continue learning and adapting our leisure beliefs to the conditions of our lifespan.

Building leisure beliefs into adult value systems is a challenge many times greater than the education of young children. During the adult years, responsibilities of family, career, and social duties in one's community occupy one's time and resources to the extent that there is little time left for reflection on one's life course. Examination of leisure beliefs and changing recreation activities requires time and effort. However, it is precisely this period of contemplation and reflection that will add vitality to one's life. Workaholics, those people who are compulsively devoted to work obligations, commonly exhibit a lack of imagination and outstanding productivity. Workaholics rarely rise above a middle management position because they are unable to reflect on the larger directions of their life and revitalize their imagination not only towards work but towards their leisure. Perhaps one way to build a leisure belief would be to hold clinics on how to cease being a workaholic in a manner similar to the how to stop smoking, drinking, or eating clinics.

Adult education programs sponsored by public schools, community colleges and universities, religious organizations, and other institutions and agencies provide another possible means to develop adult leisure beliefs. Normally these programs offer a variety of recreation classes that emphasize activity skills ranging from hobbies and games to sports and physical activities. Unfortunately, the sole focus of these classes is skill acquisition, and no time is taken to discuss leisure values or the benefits derived from the activity. These kinds of discussions should be a part of every adult education course and, if encouraged, would add greatly to the building of strong leisure beliefs in adults.

This belief-building process could be greatly enhanced by

linking leisure education topics with those courses involved in high school completion, training, retraining, and continuing professional education programs. It is extremely important for a person who is involved in enhancing career opportunities, or perhaps considering a new career or a change in the present career, to also consider the recreation activities associated with that career. Many times a change of jobs will result in different times and monetary resources available to the person, and satisfaction derived from using these resources for recreation is just as important as satisfaction derived from the new job. Certainly, any program designed to upgrade adult occupational skills should include some component of leisure either through a separate course or through discussion of leisure topics in the current course offerings.

Jean Mundy, in her model of leisure education, suggests a number of leisure beliefs that are desirable for adults.[4] Integration of personal leisure goals and attitudes into the family unit is one of the more important beliefs she discusses. Family life requires cooperation and compromise in order to achieve a harmonious mix of recreation activities that can strengthen a family unit. It is extremely important that adults maintain an attitude of positive recreation in order to build strong, positive family ties. In the process of achieving this desirable family mix of recreation activities, it is the duty of the parents to expose the family to a wide variety of leisure choices. It is also their responsibility to help insure that recreation opportunities are available not only in the home but also in the local community environment. This attitude of fostering recreation as an important part of family living is a belief that must be encouraged strongly in our society due to the tremendous pressures now being exerted upon the family unit.

Preretirement counseling is an area that offers great opportunity for building adult leisure beliefs. It has become extremely popular with large firms, which attempt to prepare their employees for the realities of retirement. A majority of the topics

---

[4]Mundy, Jean and Linda Odum. *Leisure Education: Theory and Practice.* New York. John Wiley and Sons. 1979.

addressed in these preretirement sessions concern personal finance management, health, nutrition, and various social support systems available to the elderly. More attention needs to be given to the role recreation activities can play in meeting the financial, physical, and social needs of the retired person. People of retirement age are likely to possess a strong work ethic and regard recreation as an unworthy activity. This attitude needs to be countered with a more positive outlook at the potential benefits recreation has to offer. Obviously, a positive attitude is more likely to be adopted if it is encouraged before an employee retires. Most studies of the recreation patterns exhibited by elderly persons suggest that these people continue those recreation activities in retirement that they had been enjoying while working. Many large firms are considering beginning preretirement counseling as early as the age of forty-five in order to help the employees establish positive recreation attitudes through a repertoire of activities they will be able to carry with them into their retirement years.

Making adult educators more aware of leisure education is also extremely important. Every college adult education curriculum should contain a course that addresses the needs of adults in leisure. Support for adult educators should come from a number of allied educators, including the National Recreation and Park Association. This association with its "Life—Be In It" campaign that encourages adults to adopt a more active leisure attitude should also begin offering workshops and other coordinated efforts that would encourage adult educators to emphasize the importance of leisure in their teaching. The U.S. Department of Education is extremely lacking in its efforts towards leisure education. The current Reagan administration has made several attempts to dilute the meaning of leisure in Public Law 94–142, which mandates leisure education for the handicapped. Much could be done by the Department of Education emphasizing adult education through its publication of brochures, support of research, and sponsorship of training seminars.

In summary, a systematic effort toward adult leisure education by adult educators, professional recreators, government, and our education institutions is an important need in our society. Adult leisure beliefs require examination in their relation to overall life satisfaction. Efforts should be made to help adults build those beliefs that will be most beneficial to them. As our population ages and the number of retired individuals rises, a more favorable climate towards examination of positive leisure beliefs will become evident. However until adult educators become convinced of the value of leisure, especially in relationship to the value of work, very little leadership and very little action will be seen in this area. Perhaps the ultimate solution in establishing strong adult leisure beliefs is to begin by educating the children, and then hopefully adult education will respond to the growing needs.

COMMUNITY ORGANIZATION PATTERNS

The development of a leisure ethic and value system is the beginning of a sound leisure learning program for adults. This must be supplemented and supported by an organizational pattern that will meet the needs of all adults at their level. To do this, some community-oriented agency governed by a council could be defined and instituted to coordinate and direct the leisure learning opportunities of adults. Peterson[5] suggests that a unit called Community Lifelong Learning Council (CLLC) could be defined to coordinate much of adult learning in a given community including Adult Basic Education, General Educational Development preparation, vocational-technical education, continuing professional education as well as those experiences devoted to effective leisure use.

An important function of the CLLC-type council would be to coordinate all available resources in a given community and provide communication among and between all providers of leisure learning experiences. Peterson states that "the ultimate purpose of the council would be to orchestrate learning re-

---

[5]Peterson, Richard E. and associates, *Lifelong Learning in America*, San Francisco, Jossey-Bass Publishers, 1979.

sources in the area in order to maximize participation of community people in learning activities that effectively meet their needs.'6 Although few councils of this nature do exist, they have emphasized the local planning and organizing concept to meet local needs and do have the potential to become very productive in meeting local needs.

Since a CLLC as perceived by Peterson is broad based for all of adult and continuing education and this text is concerned primarily with the leisure learning component, some modification of the council concept may be required. A subset of a major CLLC could be one alternative and a separate CLLC for leisure learning could be another. There are advantages to both types of organization patterns.

As a subset of a larger CLLC, greater resources can be available to the adult client in leisure exploration, and more adult needs, other than just leisure, can be met. If an adult client wished help in vocational–technical, adult basic education or continuing professional education and leisure education, the client can receive assistance under one theoretical roof. Further, adults interested in vocational-technical, adult basic education, and/or continuing professional education could have a much-needed exposure and some counseling in effective leisure use also. These people may need effective leisure assistance as much or more as those solely seeking leisure help. The concept of a coordinating council is to provide help to all people from the very beginning stage of awareness to the stage of meaningful leisure fulfillment.

The second alternative of a CLLC-type concept solely devoted to leisure education for adults in a given community could have the advantage of focusing only on the needs of adults in one area and could bring all attention and resources to bear on leisure. With a single purpose or goal, perhaps greater opportunities may be developed.

In either case the coordinating council can provide the leadership and direction and can be composed of members representing contributing organizations and agencies that participate in leisure experiences for adults. A leisure education council for a

---

6Ibid. p. 434.

community can be the governing board and decision-making organ and can coordinate the needs/resources assessments, resource allocations, staffing needs, and again the needed communication dimension. This council for community planning and coordination of leisure learning should be broadly based and very open to include all interested parties. Membership can come from representatives of school districts, community colleges, colleges and universities, park districts (if such are available), cooperative extension agencies, YMCA/YWCAs, city and county governments, and other agencies and organizations who have a vested interest in leisure pursuits. The size and nature of the "community" in which the council will operate could vary from a city, to several small cities, to a county or multiple counties. The key to the size would be the needs that are present and the resources that can be brought to bear. The smaller the community the easier the management, but the larger the community the greater the resources available.

Council Functions

Several major functions can be identified to which a governing council should address its attention. An early effort should focus on a need assessment to determine the needs and interests of adults in a given community. A corollary to this, possibly coming immediately after the need assessment, would be a resource assessment to determine what resources are available in the community that can be used effectively for leisure education for adults. The need assessment perhaps should include residents in rest homes, hospitals and the like, and might include various businesses who may wish help with their employees. The resource assessment should determine not only what learning experiences are available but also such things as prerequisites, costs, and other procedural concerns. Complete data in both assessments are vital for an effective adult leisure learning program.

With these data the leisure council can then review the gaps that occur between the needs and interests and the available resources. With this analysis it can be determined which needs are not or cannot be met or the ones that are met partially. The obvious final activity for the council would then be to determine how unmet needs can be satisfied. This might entail encouraging existing agencies and organizations to expand their leisure education experiences, and/or encouraging others to develop entirely new ones. The council may have to seek out funds to help others to develop entirely new experiences. The council may have to seek out funds to help other agencies or to develop new program experiences itself. Total involvement by council members in the assessment, appraisal, and planning processes is important because the entire effort will bring to the level of awareness of the council members just what needs to be done to have an effective leisure education program for adults in a given community setting.

Administrative Design

Moving from the broad-based council and the assessment and planning activity, an effective leisure education program for adults must have an administrative structure and physical setup to fulfill the mission of the program. The exact administrative structure will again be contingent on the nature of the community and the people being served.

In a broadly-based adult and continuing education concept, the leisure education aspect would be a subset of it with appropriate administrative leadership. In a solely leisure-oriented concept, the leadership structure would be obvious. In either case, the exact structure must be defined to carry out the necessary activities. In a large city perhaps a part of the city government such as the recreation board could handle the responsibilities. In smaller communities the city or county government could offer the leadership. The park district as found in Illinois or a community college, which is designed to provide many services to adults, could provide the structure and facilities for such activities. Other agencies such as YMCAs, YWCAs, regional colleges and universities, or other service organizations may also be viable solutions to the management of such adult leisure education experiences.

The staffing of the organization is critical to fulfill its mission. Highly trained professionals in leisure use and recreational activities should be present. This would include leisure counselors to help adults determine what is important to the adults and what they want from leisure. The development of leisure awareness and leisure values by adult clients would be an important function of the counselor within a given center. The use of paraprofessionals and volunteers could round out the staff. The paraprofessionals could deliver selected services to adults in the form of direct instruction, help in self-directed learning, and other guidance activities. The volunteer too could help with direct instruction and self-directed learning and could provide help with clerical and administrative duties. In fact, the development of a cadre of volunteers to assist in adult leisure learning experiences could be a worthwhile activity by the given organization. Many people are willing and able to help on a voluntary basis, and with special training these people could teach others many things in the recreation and hobby areas.

LEISURE SERVICES

A community-based adult leisure learning center can provide a number of services designed to enhance the quality of life for adult clients. A leisure exploration service can be defined to focus on adult needs and provide information about existing activities and recreational opportunities in and around the given community. Specifically this service could facilitate adult exploration of personal needs, attitudes, and obstacles toward the use of time for personal well-being, and facilitate the development of decision-making skills for self-determination in leisure. Further, this service can increase the adult clients' awareness of opportunities available to them through an effective information system.

An information referral system can be developed that could list the numerous recreational opportunities within a given area that can be used by adults. This would include actual physical sites, such as parks, rivers, and lakes; human resources, such as available consultants and volunteer helpers; available formal and informal classes in the area; and a variety of printed and other materials for adult use. A personal visit or phone call could bring the adult client the kind of assistance that is desired.

In addition to the informational service provided for those adults who have some notion about what they wish to do within the leisure domain, an awareness and individual counseling dimension should be defined to assist others less sure. Workshops can be conducted to aid adults in value clarification, time management, and decision making about personal leisure development. At these sessions adult clients can review their present status and begin to make some decisions about what is important to them. Then alternatives may be defined so that adults can try them to see if they can live a more fulfilling life-style. Individual one-on-one leisure counseling could also be instituted to explore an adult's own needs and interests and again to arrive at some alternatives for implementation. In either group or individual exploration and decision making, the emphasis should be on education—educating adults to the values of good leisure use and effective life-styling—and counseling—helping adults explore the values, make some decisions, and define some alternatives. Part of this activity would be to address personal barriers to leisure fulfillment and how one may overcome them.

An effective and as comprehensive as possible materials center should be developed and maintained. The resource materials can be used for formal and informal classes and for the self-directed adult learner. The nature of the clientele and their needs and interests would dictate the nature and quantity of materials. A catalog system of materials available at the center as well as those accessible elsewhere should be maintained to assist adults in their discovering new leisure pursuits. A delivery system for those adults who may have transportation problems should also be available.

Another function of the community leisure education center is that of public relations. The public must be aware of what the center concept is and what it can do for all adults. All available forms of media should be utilized, and an outreach program should be instituted. In the latter case personnel from the center should go to the community with slide-show presentations and other media techniques and raise the level of awareness for all adult clients. Even some group and individual counseling sessions could be conducted.

A final function of a given leisure learning center and its staff is the evaluation of programs and services. Evaluation should occur to give data for improving programs, services, and planning strategies and for instituting some accountability measures. Evaluation should be continuous and ongoing to provide some formative information so that decision makers will have some sound notions as to where changes may be made and where program modification and improvement might take place. Goals, policies, individual classes, materials, instructional strategies as well as programs and services must be subjected to careful evaluation to see if the leisure needs of adults are being met. Only with built-in and accepted measures of assessment can the staff be reasonably sure that a static situation is not present and that improvement in the life-styles of adult clients is being accomplished. Evaluation can answer the question, "Are adults feeling better about themselves and their life-styles?" This would offer a check to ascertain if leisure learning is effective in improving the quality of life for adults.

SELECTED BIBLIOGRAPHY

Apps, Jerald W., *Problems in Continuing Education*. New York, McGraw-Hill Book Company, 1980.

Brightbill, Charles K. and Tony Mobley, *Education for Leisure Centered Living*, 2nd ed., New York, John Wiley and Sons, 1977.

Cross, K. Patricia, John R. Valley and Associates, *Planning Non-Traditional Programs. An Analysis of Issues for Post Secondary Education*, San Francisco, Jossey-Bass Publishers, 1976.

Harrington, Fred Harvey, *The Future of Adult Education*, San Francisco, Jossey-Bass Publishers, 1977.

Heimstra, Roger, *Lifelong Learning*, Lincoln, Nebraska, Professional Educators Publication, Inc., 1976.

Ilsey, Paul J. and John Niemi, *Recruiting and Training Volunteers*, New York, McGraw-Hill for the Adult Education Association/U.S.A., 1981.

Kaplan, Max, *Leisure, Lifestyle, and Lifespan: Directions for Gerontology*, Philadelphia, Saunders, 1978.

Kraus, Richard, *Recreation and Leisure in Modern Society*, Santa Monica, CA, Goodyear Publishing Co., 1978.

Langerman, Philip D. and Douglas H. Smith (eds.), *Managing Adult and Continuing Education Programs and Staff*. Washington, DC, National Association for Public

Continuing and Adult Education, 1979.

Mundy, Jean and Linda Odum, *Leisure Education: Theory and Practice*, New York, John Wiley and Sons, 1979.

Parker, J. Stanley, *The Future of Work and Leisure*, New York, Praeger Publishers, 1971.

Peters, John M., *Building an Effective Adult Education Enterprise*, San Francisco, Jossey-Bass Publishers, 1980.

Peterson, Richard E. and Associates, *Lifelong Learning in America*, San Francisco, Jossey-Bass Publishers, 1979.

Verduin, John R, Jr., Harry G. Miller, and Charles E. Greer, *Adults Teaching Adults: Principles and Strategies*, Austin, TX, Learning Concepts, 1977.

APPENDIX

Introduction

THE FOLLOWING APPENDIX CONTAINS MATERIALS USED in a small group workshop that helps people explore their leisure patterns and values. The workshop is divided into three sessions, each of approximately two hours duration. The sessions are described with an activity guide sheet and a variety of handouts. Following the materials for the last session, a leader's guide to processing each individual activity is included. The workshops were developed for college students in groups of approximately twelve to fifteen. Therefore some of the individual handouts will need modification for adult groups. The rank order questions in Session II and the leisure assertiveness scale and leisure auction list in Session III would need changes.

The workshop format and sequence of activities are based on general group dynamic principles and techniques. For best results a group leader must be trained in these skills in order to facilitate group discussion. Many group leaders were trained at the masters level. However, the Leisure Exploration Service had good success in training undergraduate students as paraprofessional leaders. Such training can be completed in a reasonable time frame of approximately twenty hours. One strong advantage of utilizing peer group leaders is the great rapport that can be built with group participants. Many times such a rapport opens the discussion and facilitates real sharing of thoughts and values.

The authors would like to acknowledge the many persons who

139

were responsible for developing the materials in this appendix. In principle, Cathy Rankin, who has been with the Leisure Exploration Service since its inception, was instrumental in setting the workshop philosophy. Ed Leoni and Doctors Linda Bernard and Beverly Brown were also deeply involved in the design and implementation of the workshop materials. For more information concerning materials and activities of the Leisure Exploration Service please contact:

Ms. Cathy Rankin
Office of Intramural–Recreational Sports
Southern Illinois University
Carbondale, IL 62901
PH: (618) 536–5531

LEISURE AWARENESS WORKSHOP

Session I

Approx. Time

10 min.   I. Introduction: Introduce Leisure Exploration Service, purpose and overview of workshop. Brief discussion on individuals' philosophy of leisure.

20 min.   II. Introductory Exercise (Icebreaker) (If group is less than 10)
   A. Purpose/Goal: To give participants the opportunity to get to know each other and feel at ease with each other.
   B. Process: Use an exercise of your choice, i.e. Split large groups into pairs and have them introduce each other and tell a little about themselves and what they like to do in their leisure. Then the partners will introduce each other to the rest of the group.

30 min.   III. Initial Assessment of Leisure Values
   A. Twenty Things I Love To Do
      1. Material Utilized: Twenty Things I Love To Do Worksheet and pencils.
      2. Purpose/Goal: To help the participants examine their most prized and cherished leisure values and activities.
      3. Process: Group members will fill out the worksheet individually. At the completion of the exercise participants will share what they learned about their leisure values and process the exercise in dyads, then with the entire group.

   IV. Values Clarification Exercises
   A. Pie of Life
      1. Materials Utilized: Pie of Life Worksheet and pencil.

2. Purpose/Goal: To allow participants to see the organizational patterns of their present leisure time.
3. Process: Group members will fill out the worksheet individually.
    a) Members will fill in the times when they sleep, have classes, or other obligations.
    b) The remaining time periods will be considered free time.
    c) Processing will focus on the utilization of the free time hours. Members will process in dyads, followed by group discussion.

20–25 min.   B. Open-ended Questions
1. Materials Utilized: Open-ended Questions Worksheet and pencil.
2. Purpose/Goal. To allow participants to explore patterns in their thoughts and activities.
3. Process: The participants will process patterns of attitudes and behaviors in the group.

20 min.   V. Guided Fantasy
A. Worksheet available in your packet. Have the group get comfortable and close their eyes. Once the group is relaxed, lead them toward their perfect leisure fantasy. Process the fantasy in dyads, encouraging the group to share feelings they experienced and some of the differences between their fantasy and their real life.
B. Process:
1. This activity is designed to allow participants to experience leisure as a *State Of Mind*!!!
2. In order for the experience to be effective you must:

    a) Be relaxed yourself.
    b) Do not become hurried.
    c) Be comfortable with silence and long pauses.
3. Realize that this experience comes in two phases. First is the relaxation phase and second is the actual guided fantasy phase.
4. The purpose of this exercise is to experience a significant place or event of great meaning for the participants so as to activate the *feelings* of "leisure" as a state of mind.

TWENTY THINGS I LOVE TO DO

	1	2	3	4	5	6
1.						
2.						
3.						
4.						
5.						
6.						
7.						
8.						
9.						
10.						
11.						
12.						
13.						
14.						
15.						
16.						
17.						
18.						
19.						
20.						

- Put letter A after activities you like to do alone; P after those you enjoy doing with people, and AP by those you enjoy doing either alone or with people.
- Put a dollar sign ($) after all the activities that cost at least four dollars or more each time you do them.
- Put N5 after those activities you would not have had on your list five years ago.
- Put PL next to the activities that need planning. (Use your personal definition of planning.)
- After each activity, indicate when you last did it (month or year).

· Put a check (✔) beside those things your friends usually initiate.

PIE OF LIFE

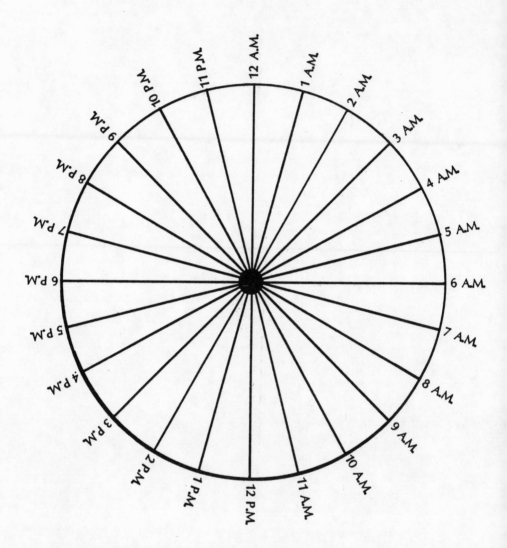

OPEN–ENDED QUESTIONS RELATED TO LEISURE AND VALUES

1. If this next weekend were a three-day weekend, I would want to ...
2. My bluest days are ...
3. I've made up my mind to finally learn how to ...
4. If I could get a free subscription to two magazines, I would select ... Because ...
5. I feel most bored when ...
6. If I used my free time more wisely, I would ...
7. I feel proud most when ...
8. Socializing offers me a chance to ...
9. If I had no television, I would ...
10. The next rainy day I plan to ...
11. On Saturdays I like to ...
12. If I had a tankful of gas in a car ...
13. I feel best when people ...
14. On vacations, I like to ...
15. I'd like to tell my best friend ...
16. The happiest day in my life was ...
17. My favorite vacation place would be ...
18. My best friend can be counted on to ...
19. I am best at ...
20. In a group I am ...
21. People who agree with me make me feel ...
22. When people depend on me, I ...
23. I get angry when ...
24. I have accomplished ...
25. I get real pleasure from ...
26. People who expect a lot from me make me feel ...
27. The things that amuse me most are ...
28. I feel warmest toward a person when ...
29. If I feel I can't get across to another person ...
30. What I want most in life is ...
31. I am ...
33. People who know me well think I am ...
34. My greatest strength is ...
35. I need to improve most in ...

36. I would consider it risky...
37. When people first meet me, they...
38. In a group, I am most afraid when...
39. I feel closest to someone when...
40. I feel loved most when...
41. I have never liked...
42. I feel happiest of all when...
43. When my family gets together...
44. I like people who...
45. The trouble with being honest is...
46. The trouble with being dishonest is...
47. Someday I am going to...
48. When my friends suggest a leisure activity, I...
49. I don't have enough time to...
50. My greatest accomplishment in leisure has been...
51. My favorite hiding place is...

GUIDED FANTASY EXERCISE

The following outline is a guide for you to use in leading a guided fantasy experience. It is only meant as an aid and should not be read word for word.

I. Relaxation Phase—participants must feel relaxed in order to fully gain something from the experience.
   A. Find a comfortable position, either your chairs or on the floor. (Pause)
   B. It is most helpful if you close your eyes and allow yourself to get in the experience of a total way. (Pause)
   C. Be aware of your surroundings. Know the building you are in; the room you are in; and the people around you.
   D. Let everything go! Let the outside sounds drift by and begin to focus on *yourself*. (Pause)
   E. Begin to focus on your breathing. Be aware of inhalation and exhalation of breath. Watch your cycle of breath go in and out, in and out. (Pause)
   F. Be aware of your body. Feel the contact of your body with the chair or floor. Feel where the tension in your body is. Feel the tenseness and release it...let it go. (Pause)
   G. Continue to be aware of your breathing... Follow it in and out... Inhalation and exhalation... (Pause)

II. Fantasy Phase—slowly move into assisting the participant to move into their respective fantasy. Do not plant specific ideas in their fantasy, but give them plenty of free space to roam.
   A. Begin to move into the place you want to be in your fantasy. (Pause)
   B. Be aware of the surroundings in this place. What does it look like there? (Pause)
   C. What does it *feel* like to be in this place? (Pause)
   D. Are you with other people... or alone? (Pause)
   E. What does it *feel* like to be with these people/or to be alone? (Pause)
   F. Be aware of the smells, sights and sounds at this place. What are they like? (Pause)

G. Begin to be aware of your breathing once again. Inhalation and exhalation . . . In and out . . . (Pause)
H. Slowly and at your relaxed pace, begin to pull out of your fantasy and return to the group.
I. Take your time, do not hurry! Slowly open your eyes and pull back with us!

LEISURE AWARENESS WORKSHOP

Session II

Approx. Time

20–30 min.

III. Introductory Exercise:
   A. Material Utilized: Paper and pencil.
   B. Purpose/Goal: To allow participants to explore how others perceive them and their leisure activities.
   C. Process: Each group member will draw a picture of themselves in their leisure. Once the pictures are completed the members will pass the picture around the group with each group member writing a word or phrase the picture suggests to them about the person who drew it. After each person in the group has seen the picture, return it to its owner and process the results in the group.

20 min.

II. Values Clarification
   A. Rank Order Questions
      1. Material Utilized: Rank Order Questions Worksheet and pencil.
      2. Purpose/Goal: To allow individuals to explore their leisure values and priorities.
      3. Process: Group members will individually complete the Rank Order Questions. Members will process results in dyads, followed by group discussion.

20–30 min.

III. Making Changes
   A. Perfect Day
      1. Material Utilized: Pie of Life Worksheet and pencil.
      2. Purpose/Goal: To help members orga-

nize and utilize their time as they would ideally like it.
3. Process:
    a) Participants will construct an ideal 24 hours. This will include what they will be doing, who they will be with, where they will be, and any other pertinent details.
    b) This perfect day will be compared to actual days and processed group discussion.
    c) The two Pies of Life will be considered along with a discussion of the elements and feelings that make up a balanced life-style.

30 min.   B. Decision Making
    1. Materials Utilized: Decision Making handout and alternatives sheet.
    2. Purpose/Goal: To familiarize participants with steps in decision making and provide the opportunity to utilize these steps.
    3. Process:
        a) This is done in conjunction with the Alternatives Sheet.
        b) Go over steps in decision making (they already have alternatives listed).
        c) Have participants go through steps they will need to take in order to implement their commitment.
        d) Give time to choose alternative.

5–10 min.   IV. Commitment to Group
    A. Each member will choose one of the alternative activities and make a commitment to the group that they will try the activity before the next session. Members will share successes or barriers they encoun-

tered at the next session. (It is also permissable to allow someone to not make a commitment.)

RANK ORDER QUESTIONS

Directions: Rank the following in order of preference
  1. Where would you rather be on a Saturday afternoon?
             at the beach
             in the woods
             in a discount store
  2. Which season do you like best?
             winter
             summer
             spring
             fall
  3. Which do you least like to do?
             listen to a Beethoven symphony
             watch a debate
             watch a play
  4. Which would you most like to improve?
             your looks
             the way you use your time
             your social life
  5. How do you have the most fun?
             alone
             with a large group
             with a few friends
             with your family
  6. If you had two hours to spend with a friend, which would you do?
             stand on a corner
             go to a movie
             go for a walk
             go bowling
  7. If you suddenly inherited money and became a millionaire, would you—
             share your wealth through charities, education trust funds, etc.
             continue in your present job and activities
             really live it up
  8. If you had $10 extra that you did not need for something else, would you—

        save it

        treat a friend (or family member) to dinner

        buy a new record

9. Which do you like best?

        winter in the mountains

        summer by the sea

        autumn in the country

10. In your leisure time, what would you most like to do?

        weave, make pottery, or do some craft

        play the piano

        play tennis

11. Which do you like to do most?

        play football

        play golf

        swim

12. Which would you like to do most?

        learn to skin dive

        learn to ride a motor bike

        learn to ride a horse

13. How would you spend an inheritance?

        on travel

        on education

        on entertainment

14. What would you most like to do with your friends during your leisure time?

        play a sport or game

        go to a movie or watch T.V.

        just talk

        play cards

15. Which of these problems do you think is the greatest threat in the near future?

        overpopulation

        too much leisure time

        water and air pollution

        crime

16. How would you rather spend a Saturday evening?

        at a good play

        at a good concert

_____ at a good movie
17. How would you rather spend a Saturday evening?
    _____ at a nightclub
    _____ at home alone
    _____ at a party at a friend's home
18. Which would you rather do on your birthday?
    _____ spend it at home with family
    _____ ignore it
    _____ go out to dinner
19. What would you rather be able to do well?
    _____ dance
    _____ sing
    _____ draw
20. What would you most like to see built in your neighborhood?
    _____ a swimming pool
    _____ tennis courts
    _____ a park

PIE OF LIFE

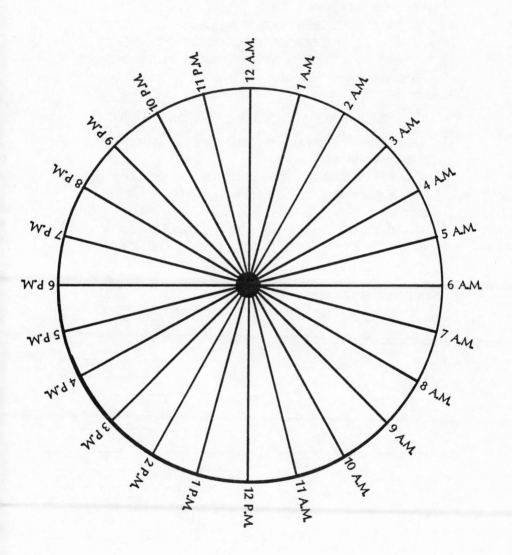

STEPS IN DECISION MAKING

1. Prepare a list of alternatives.
2. Imagine the outcome of each alternative.
3. Consider past experience in similar situations.
4. Evaluate the outcome of each alternative in terms of desirability.
5. Select a course of action.
6. Act.

QUESTIONS TO ASK IN DECISION MAKING

1. What are the different possible courses of action I might take in this situation?
2. What will be the consequences of each course of action?
3. What experiences in the past will help me select a course of action?
4. What outcome is most desirable as far as I am concerned?
5. What course of action is the most appropriate for me?

ALTERNATIVES

List 3 possible changes in your life for next week	Pros	Cons
1. _____	_____	_____
2. _____	_____	_____
3. _____	_____	_____

LEISURE AWARENESS WORKSHOP

Session III

Approx. Time

20–30 min.   I. Group Sharing Exercise
A. Each group member will share their experience with the activity they committed themselves to do in the previous session. Members will be encouraged to talk about the activity, as well as some of their feelings and how this experience might affect future commitments.

30 min.   II. Barriers to Change
A. Materials Utilized: Barriers to Change Worksheet and pencil.
B. Purpose/Goal: To help participants anticipate some of the barriers they will face in implementing changes and deal with steps to overcome them.
C. Process: As a group, the participants will list perceived or real barriers that keep them from doing activities. They will also collectively list steps that can be taken to reduce or overcome these barriers.

30 min.   III. Leisure Assertiveness Self-Scale
A. Materials Utilized: Leisure Assertiveness Self-Scale and pencil.
B. Purpose/Goal: To raise awareness of the following:
1. Assertive issues and rights in leisure.
2. Leisure values as they compare to work and inter– and intrapersonal areas.
3. Discovering barriers, constraints, and irrational beliefs that may inhibit leisure pursuits.

           C. Process: Group members will individually complete the Self-Scale. Assertiveness areas will be talked about, and group discussion will follow.

20 min.   IV. Leisure Auction

           A. Material Utilized: List of leisure activities and pencil.

           B. Purpose/Goal: To assess some leisure values and their worth to the individuals.

           C. Process: Each participant will have 10 imaginary dollars to spend on the auction. The items listed will be auctioned off to the group. Each participant can note which activities they wish to bid on and the probable amount they will bid on their activities sheet. There are two BONUS items. After bidding and when winners have been decided on, they will be told what they receive (BONUS #11 is free belly dancing lessons; BONUS #17 is a moonlight skinny dip with the person of your choice.)

10 min.   V. Evaluation

           A. Material Utilized: Evaluation Worksheet and pencil.

           B. Purpose/Goal: To evaluate the workshop experience, including strengths and weaknesses of the workshop exercises.

           C. Process: Participants will individually fill out the evaluation questionnaire and return the completed worksheet to the facilitator.

OVERCOMING BARRIERS

Barriers	Steps to Overcome Them

GUIDE TO
LEISURE ASSERTIVENESS WORKSHEET

The worksheet questions pertain to the following areas of assertiveness:

1–4	Standing up for your rights
5–9	Initiating social situations
10–15	Refusing requests
16–20	Saying no to close friends

LEISURE SELF--ASSERTIVE SCALE

1	2	3	4	5
Never or Rarely	Seldom	Sometimes	Usually	Almost Always

1. When planning with a group of friends I _____ offer my ideas and we _____ do what I suggest.
2. A talkative neighbor drops by while I am listening to music. I would _____ ask them to come back later.
3. A group of friends have planned a picnic. I learned that they want to invite a couple I don't like very much. I would _____ bring up this issue.
4. I have made plans for the weekend. My parents call and tell me they have made plans to visit me. I would _____ ask them to cancel their plans.
5. If the dance floor was empty I would _____ be the first one to start dancing.
6. While viewing a live game I _____ will initiate a conversation with a stranger sitting next to me.
7. I have come up with this great plan for the weekend, but I think my friends will think it's corny. I will _____ say it anyway.
8. I am at an outdoor activity and the M.C. asks for a volunteer from the audience. I would _____ volunteer.
9. I told a friend I would attend his party. At the last moment I decide not to go. I would _____ call him.
10. If my parents come down for the weekend, I _____ say where we will go.
11. If an acquaintance asks me to go out on a school night I _____ say no.
12. Two little persons ask me to be their scout master or else they will lose their eligibility. I am exceptionally busy this semester. I would _____ say no.
13. I have planned a full day of recreation for Saturday. A neighbor wants to know if I would like to finish the fence we started building. I would _____ say sorry, leisure first.
14. The president of a club on campus asks me to attend one of

their meetings. I would _____ tell him I am not interested.

15. A professor asks me to join the department team in a sport I am not very good at and have little interest in. I would _____ refuse.

16. If a good friend asks me to go uptown for a beer on a school night I would _____ say no.

17. If a new friend were to ask to borrow my new tennis racquet I would _____ ask him to give me time to use it first.

18. If I am home fixing a dinner I wanted very much and a close friend calls saying he has gone to great lengths to reserve a racquetball court I would _____ tell him my dinner was more important.

19. A good friend does not like to go uptown alone. He/she calls me during my study time. I would _____ say no, I am committed to study time.

20. I have decided to spend all of Friday alone. My best friend calls and says he/she is really bored and wants to do something/anything. I would _____ tell him/her maybe some other time.

LEISURE AUCTION ACTIVITY LIST

1. $_____ Racquet court reserved for 2 hours per week for 1 month.
2. $_____ Fishing trip in Canada for 1 week.
3. $_____ An all-expenses paid evening at the bar of your choice.
4. $_____ A season pass for any sporting event.
5. $_____ A month of diversified outdoor activities.
6. $_____ Rubber raft trip down the Current River.
7. $_____ Free concert tickets for one concert in Carbondale and one in St. Louis.
8. $_____ An expenses-paid weekend in St. Louis.
9. $_____ Free lessons for instrument of your choice.
10. $_____ Free lessons for sport of your choice.
11. $_____ BONUS
12. $_____ Free rent of color T.V. for 3 months.
13. $_____ Free trip to King Tut exhibit.
14. $_____ Free meals from nutritional buffet for 1 month.
15. $_____ A $100 shopping spree.
16. $_____ Free dance lessons.
17. $_____ BONUS

GROUP LEADER'S GUIDE FOR
PROCESSING WORKSHOP EXERCISES

Twenty Things I Love To Do

1. Explore any trends you see about your leisure life-style.
2. Did you notice anything new or did this exercise reaffirm some of the things you already knew about yourself.
3. Look at the things that cost money. Did you find more or less of these than you expected? What does this mean to you?
4. What about the N5 column. Have you remained the same over the past 5 years? How do you feel about the results of this?
5. Have you done the things you listed recently? Explore the significance of your responses.
6. Are you mostly involved in activities your friends suggest? How do you feel about your own assertiveness when it pertains to leisure?
7. Do you find you do things alone or with people?

Pie of Life (Ideal Day)

1. Look at the elements that make up a balanced life-style. Collectively list these, and list the associated feelings.
2. Do you see a balance in your present life-style in your ideal day?
3. Remember the feelings you experienced in the Guided Fantasy. Try to explore if those feelings are associated with your ideal day.
4. Explore the possibilities of fitting a portion or even an hour of your ideal day into your typical day.
5. Would you like to share your ideal day?

Pie of Life (Typical Day)

1. What is the most outstanding thing you see from your Pie of Life?
2. Do you see a balance in your present life-style? Explain.
3. What changes would you like to make in your typical day?

Rank Order Questions

1. Think back to the previous exercises. What trends do you see continuing in this exercise, especially those you chose as #1.
2. Do you see any pattern to your #1 responses, such as mostly with people or mostly outdoor activities, etc.

3. Was there a question that caught your attention or was hard to answer?
4. Explore any questions that surprised you when you responded to them.
5. Are there questions you would like to explore further and see how others in the group responded?
6. Have the participants leave the last three blank. They can exchange papers with another person and determine how close they can come to what the other person is like through their responses. Then the partners can answer the last three questions the way they think the other person would have ranked them, based on the other responses.

Open-ended Questions

1. What question was hardest to answer spontaneously?
2. Did you find any surprises in your answers?
3. How do your responses fit into a pattern with the other exercises we have done?
4. Was there a question you could *not* answer?
5. Explore with the group any questions you would like to know other responses.
6. Would anyone like to share some of their completed sentences.
7. Did you notice any pattern to your answers?

Guided Fantasy

1. Would anyone like to share their fantasy?
2. What feelings do you identify in your fantasy?
3. How is your fantasy different from your real life?
4. What does your fantasy tell you about yourself?
5. Is it important to fantasize about leisure?

Draw Yourself in Leisure Exercise

1. What do you think about some of the comments about your picture?
2. Are the comments accurate? Do they fit for you?
3. Is your perception of yourself similar to others perception of you?
4. Do you like your leisure self?

Decision Making Exercise

1. What did you find yourself doing while trying to make a decision (alternatives, good and bad outcome, etc.)?
2. Is it difficult to make a decision and stick to it? Why?
3. How do you normally explore the alternatives in making a decision or is it spontaneous?
4. Do you think about things internally or externally?

Group Sharing Exercise

1. Did you keep the commitment you made to the group? Why or why not?
2. What events and thoughts influenced your decision?
3. How do you feel doing that activity or inactivity?
4. Does the activity help you to feel better about yourself?

Barriers to Decision Making Exercise

1. It seems like we all have some barriers that keep us from doing what we want. I am wondering if these are all real or just perceived blocks.
2. What kinds of things do we tell ourselves that build up these barriers?
3. What are some things you might do to remove some of those barriers to doing what you want?

Assertiveness Exercise

1. What is the difference between assertive, nonassertive, and aggressive communications or actions?
2. What might be some benefits to being an assertive person as compared to passive or aggressive?
3. What have you found out about yourself? What patterns appear in the way you do things? Did you already know that or is it new information?
4. What do you want to do about the way you are?

Auction Exercise

1. Does anyone want to tell us where they spent most of their money?
2. What have we found out about each others' values?
3. Are you comfortable with your expenditures?

INDEX